# STRENGTH TRAINING
# FOR ATHLETES

# STRENGTH TRAINING
# FOR ATHLETES

## Michael A. Winch

**FOREWORD BY JUDY OAKES OBE**

CROWOOD

First published in 2004 by
The Crowood Press Ltd
Ramsbury, Marlborough
Wiltshire SN8 2HR

**www.crowood.com**

**British Library Cataloguing-in-Publication Data**
A catalogue record for this book is available from the British Library.

ISBN 1 86126 650 2

All illustrations are by the author, except where otherwise credited. Many
thanks to Dan Grossman, Howard Payne and Mark Shearman of Athletics
Images (athleticsimages@aol.com) for supplying photographs for use in
the book.

Typeset by NBS Publications, Basingstoke, Hampshire, RG21 5NH

Printed and bound in Great Britain by Stanley L. Hunt Ltd, Rushton

# Contents

# Foreword

Strength training has been part of my life since I started athletics back in the early 1970s. At that time I asked Mike Winch whether he would coach me. Little did I know what this was to entail. He immediately put me on a strength training programme working out in the gym at the Crystal Palace National Sports Centre. At the time few women athletes trained there, but I soon overcame my anxieties, learning what real hard work was.

I never looked back, my strength and shot putting continuing to improve steadily year by year. The schedules that Mike set were difficult and testing, but, applying the principles laid out in this book, I was able to achieve many championship wins in three sports, track and field, weight lifting and power lifting.

When I started in sport I was told that I was too small to be a thrower, but with Mike's efforts and my own doggedness success came. It was a success for simple principles applied correctly, which is the main aim of this book. Any young athlete or coach can start on the road to achievement by thoroughly understanding strength training and how it can be applied to all sports and athletic events.

Strength training is at the very heart of all athletic events, and perseverance in the gym will bring great rewards, not only in terms of results but also in remaining injury-free. From the marathon runner to the discus thrower, strength will help in the achievement of a long career and competitive success.

This book explains simply how to achieve the best results by setting up a strength programme as part of the overall training plan, and it is this consistent and safe approach to the subject, combined with well-thought-out preparation, that leads to the very best improvements.

*Strength Training for Athletes* is a must for every coach and athlete who takes his or her sport seriously. Its extensive and well explained contents are the basis of sound and safe progress in the sport.

Judy Oakes OBE

# Acknowledgements

I would like to thank my former coaches the late 'Jack' Milford, Peter Lay and Stevie Stevenson for their inspirational teaching in my days as an athlete. Also Wilf Paish and Tom McNab who have laid down the rules for coaching in this country for many years.

My own squad of athletes, who have suffered the schedules I have set and cheerfully helped in my own development as a coach, also deserve my thanks since without them I would have had nobody to experiment on.

Judy Oakes, who has been an inspiration in our sport for three decades, has helped in the compilation of this book, both in being the model for many of the photographs and also in inspiring me to work on the text. Her contribution has been great and I thank her for it.

Sir Eddie Kulukundis must be acknowledged for his wonderful help over the last twenty years. His support has been invaluable, and without it my own understanding of international athletics would have been much diminished.

Finally, I thank my wife Carole, who continually assures me that I can write something of value and my Mum, who, as a writer herself, taught me the basics at a very early age, and continues to cast her expert eye over my manuscripts.

Mike Winch BSc
*Chief Athletics Coach to the 2002 England Commonwealth Games Team*

# CHAPTER 1
# Introduction to Strength Training

'Strength training' is a term that has been used and abused over the years spanning the modern era of athletics. Many myths and misconceptions have evolved, most of which are derived from the empirical nature of training methods used, until the more recent development of sports science. Some of these misconceptions have been based on social prejudices, such as those relating to the supposed inability of women to gain strength, and the 'muscle-bound' theory, neither of which holds water when closely and scientifically examined.

The former has, of course, been proved untrue in the same way that many myths about female physiology have. It is true to say that, in the main, women are structurally and hormonally less able to build strength than men, but this does not mean that they cannot make huge gains when placed in the gymnasium with the right programmes of development. Indeed, the female body adapts to heavy strength training as it does when pressed into hard endurance activities. A strong woman can put the majority of men to shame, just as Paula Radcliffe has done in the marathon.

The latter myth, that of the high probability of becoming muscle-bound when strength training is adopted, is more a reflection of older, heavily unbalanced training programmes being used with little or no suppling or mobility work included. It is true that muscles become highly toned with strength training, and that it is vital that

no range of movement is lost, but, by working a balanced and aware programme, there is little chance of hindering the athlete, in fact, quite the reverse is true.

'Strength' is determined by the aims and objectives of the training to be performed for the required event. For example, 'strength' to a shot putter is very different from the 'strength' sought by a 5,000m runner in the last stage of the race. It is therefore most important for the coach and the athlete to understand exactly what is meant by the word and how their particular types of 'strength' are increased.

The incorrect understanding, and therefore definition, of those strengths, lies at the heart of many poor results and negative statements made about strength in sports training. The cause is often the difficulty some people experience in analysing the different facets of an extensive subject. We are all conditioned to use the word 'strength' as if it had one immutable meaning. As you read this book you may well be surprised to realize just how many meanings the word has and how diverse are the methods available for strength training. Whatever definition is used, the reason for developing the particular 'strength' needed must be to improve sporting performance. If the training does not have this effect it is either being performed wrongly or the wrong methods are being applied. There is no doubt that strength training, if done correctly, can enhance the performance of athletes in all events.

Fig. 1 Women can be strong: Judy Oakes lifting 117.5kg.

The strength training practices used today are founded on early fairground and circus strongman acts. Most of these men gained strength above their normal level by practising movements with heavy objects, which eventually evolved into dumbbells and barbells. The image of a hirsute man, dressed in a leopard skin leotard, lofting a massive barbell above his head, is one with which most of us are familiar. It was not, however, until the turn of the twentieth century that weightlifting as a sport became popular, and with it the concept of progressive resistance training, which is at the heart of modern strength-gain techniques.

At this early stage, weightlifting and the sport of track and field athletics were worlds apart. Weightlifting was based firmly in the working class, where it has remained until relatively recently. Track and field were mostly performed by the leisured classes, the only people able to afford the time to train and compete without earning money from their sport. This, of course, has now completely changed.

The significance of using weights, or at least progressive resistance work, to assist athletic performance was not realized until just before the Second World War. How and when such training started is difficult to pinpoint, but it could well have derived from the use of resistance work in the rehabilitation of the muscles of injured servicemen. As today, the major centres of development were in the USA and eastern Europe, but in each area a particular approach was adopted. In America, athletes went full pelt towards weights, with no idea as to the use or consequences of what they were doing. In Europe progress was slower and geared to the traditionally developed, specific training methods more related to athleticism than pure, brute strength.

Since those early days, when lifting heavy weights was thought to be the panacea for all events, a merging of ideas has led to the detailed and exhaustive research on which modern methods are based. The introduction of sophisticated machinery involving pulleys and cams, as well as fixed-weight stacks and hydraulics, is all part of the movement towards making it easier to gain strength without the drudgery and danger of continually loading and unloading bars. These innovations have broadened the horizons of many athletes who are now reaping the rewards of their efforts. Such machinery has also stimulated research into different types of resistance training and their relevance to the specific strengths necessary to improve athletic performance. The relative merit of constant-speed movement, as opposed to constant-resistance movement, is only one of many recent investigations that seem to be producing increasingly useful results.

The current state of the art is one of change, although the fundamental ground rules for strength gain in the several sports and events are now generally agreed. In view of this, it is puzzling that many sports coaches should be so behind in their concepts and knowledge of strength training. It is no exaggeration to say that many coaches who have athletes going to the Olympic Games have little or no knowledge of even the most rudimentary strength schedule structure, or even the limits of their athletes' strength potential. Only since about 1960 has the broad swath of coaches become aware that resistance training can benefit athletes in all sports and events. Unfortunately, even now some are blissfully unaware of the huge benefit a correctly structured strength programme can be, and still deprecate the use of such methods as having negative effects on competitors.

Recently, what has swayed opinion in a positive direction is the more extensive use of advanced strength-training methods adopted by many athletes in endurance events. The logical conclusion is that, if

Fig. 2 The power of the sprinter. (Dan Grossman)

these athletes can benefit, then so can athletes in all other events, a statement which in many countries has long been accepted and put into practice.

The purpose of this book is to enlighten those athletes and coaches who have either never learnt about strength training or who are just starting on their athletic or coaching careers. It cannot be fully comprehensive, since that would take much more space. Nevertheless, this volume is designed to give a thorough understanding of the basics of such training, together with explanations of and the reasons for doing what is suggested. There are many views on the subject and

what is put forward here is not the only right way. However, its content is based on many years of working, not only with Olympic athletes but also with beginners, laymen and women all of whom have wanted to improve their performance.

It is hoped that the following chapters will give you the motivation necessary to try new ideas and methods, as well as to go further and learn more about the subject. The results you achieve are always best when techniques and methods are performed correctly and not in an arbitrary or illogical way. The principles set out here will allow you to start your learning with confidence.

# CHAPTER 2
# Muscle Structure and Function

## MUSCLES

The muscles of the body are the basic mechanism by which the functions of the brain are expressed externally. This includes the unconscious actions that maintain our in-built, life-support systems, such as breathing and the pumping action of the heart, as well as the conscious movements resulting from the will to move. These two systems are controlled through separate nerve/muscle combinations called the involuntary (unconscious) and the voluntary (conscious) system. The muscles that are involved with each system are structurally and functionally different.

The involuntary muscles are made up of many single, non-fibrous and separate cells (Fig. 3), whereas the voluntary muscles are made up of long, thin fasciculi. These are bundles of muscle fibres, each of which is a number of individual cells that have combined structurally to form the single, fibrous unit. Each fibre has multiple nuclei but no cell boundaries dividing it into separate cells.

The most obvious, visible difference between the two types of muscle, apart from their cellular natures, is that the voluntary muscle is striped (striated). This can be seen clearly under the light microscope in most commonly eaten red meats. These stripes are an important and vital clue to the way in which the muscle works. It was not until the introduction of the electron microscope that the structure of voluntary muscle was elucidated. Before this the exact nature of the stripes and how they were part of the

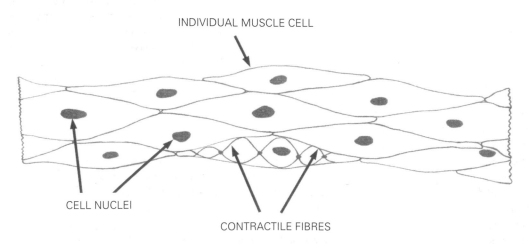

INDIVIDUAL MUSCLE CELL

CELL NUCLEI

CONTRACTILE FIBRES

Fig. 3 Smooth, involuntary muscle fibres.

contraction (shortening process) were not clear.

Detailed study and chemical analysis of the muscle fibres led to the rapid understanding of how they worked. On looking closely at the stripes we see that they are actually made up of areas of dense protein that occur regularly along the length of the muscle cell. If the fibre is examined more closely it is seen to be constructed from what are called bundles of myofibrils. Chemical analysis has shown these to be made up of mainly two proteins, actin (the transparent part) and myosin (the dense stripes).

The actin is present in the form of twisted filaments (like wool) and the myosin as bundles of parallel filaments, giving the latter a microscopically much denser nature. The myosin filaments form chemical protein links with the surrounding actin filaments. These are called muscle bridges and are the heart of the contracting process. The bridges shorten or lengthen depending on the state of the muscle. During contraction they shorten, bringing the muscle proteins closer together. This process requires energy that is supplied on the stimulus of nervous activity. The nature of this process will be discussed later.

## THE CONNECTING TISSUES

For the muscle to function, it must be attached to the bones and kept separate from the surrounding tissues. Two distinct types of connecting tissue exist to perform these tasks (Fig. 4). The tendons are the connecting tissues between the muscles and the bones. The bones act as levers within the body and enable the force produced by the muscles to be transmitted and translated into bodily movements. The tendons therefore perform a vital task. Each is made up of strands of a strong and only slightly elastic protein called collagen. This is called white

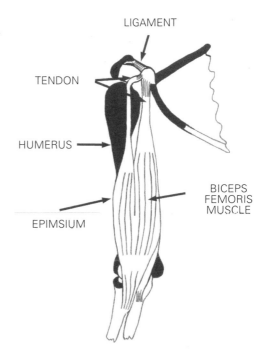

Fig. 4 The shoulder and upper arm.

fibrous tissue. At the bone end of the connection, the collagen 'sticks' to the bone, the attachment being capable of withstanding incredible stresses. At the muscle end, the tendon blends into the connecting tissue surrounding the muscle itself, and therefore has a strong and widespread attachment.

This tissue, keeping the muscle separate from its surroundings, is called the epimysium (Fig. 4) and is also mainly composed of collagen fibres (white fibrous tissue), but, being thinner, is slightly more elastic to allow the muscle to swell during exercise. Within the muscle, each fasciculum is surrounded by another sheath called the perimysium which separates the fibre bundles from one another and allows the blood and nerve supplies access to the inner parts of the muscle body. Finally, the fibres themselves are surrounded by connective tissue called endomysium, which keeps each one separate and again allows the blood and nerves to reach their final destination. The connective tissues, therefore, have a vital role to play in the mechanical functioning of the muscle and must not be overlooked in any study undertaken.

## ENERGY SYSTEMS IN MUSCULAR CONTRACTION

There has been a long and active debate about what exactly are the energy sources for muscular contraction. This was renewed when it was observed that there are two major types of muscle fibre to be found within an individual muscle. These are commonly known as the white and the red fibres and appear to have a very different structure and function. The red fibres are associated with endurance activity and are slow acting but long working. Their colour relates to the presence of many mitochondria (cellular power stations) and to oxygen-carrying myoglobin protein. The white fibres are linked to rapid action and short endurance, and it has been suggested that they are responsible for the 'cold start' mechanism of the muscle since no oxygen is utilized when they contract. These are the anaerobic fibres and there are several different types, using different balances of energy sources. The red fibres are aerobic, having a dependence on oxygen for their activity.

Although the two types of fibre both ultimately use the breakdown of adenosine triphosphate (ATP) into adenosine diphosphate (ADP) in order to contract, they have different ways of doing this, or at least different balances of the several available energy sources. The ATP breakdown causes the release of energy that produces a change in the physical shape of

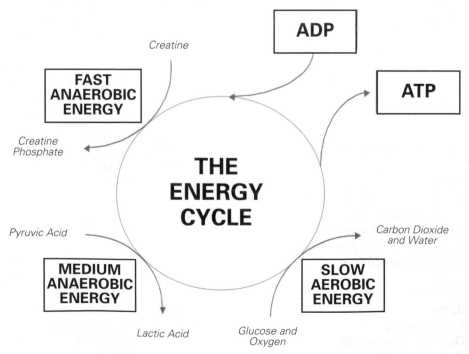

Fig. 5 The energy sources within muscle.

the muscle proteins, a sliding movement of the central myosin protein inside the surrounding actin protein, as described above. The sliding movement causes shortening of the muscle fibres and hence their contraction, which can be sustained only as long as the energy supply is available. Once the ATP runs out the muscle can no longer contract.

Taking the white (fast twitch) fibres first, it appears that, since they have few mitochondria (cell parts which are concerned with aerobic energy production), they must rely on anaerobic energy sources (Fig. 5) primarily. These include: (i) a minute store of ATP itself; (ii) stored creatine phosphate (CP), which is another high energy compound like ATP which can be converted rapidly to ATP and then reformed later from the slow, aerobic energy production system; (iii) the combination of two ADP molecules to form one of ATP and one of adenosine monophosphate; and (iv) the synthesis of new ATP by an anaerobic system involving the production of lactic acid from fatty acids, glucose or amino acid products.

The use of these rapidly available energy sources means that the white fibres can contract swiftly, but, because of the relatively small size of the stores, they can only act for a short period. Excluding the lactic acid system, the muscles can only work flat out for about 10 to 12sec effectively. This is extended at a lesser intensity for another 35 to 40sec by the creation of ATP as a result of the formation of lactic acid, that is eventually produced in such quantities that the whole body is poisoned and physical activity is reduced to a negligible level. Hence the drastic reduction in speed during the last 50m of a 400m run, particularly for a lower level athlete.

The red fibres work in a very different way. They are slow reacting (slow twitch) fibres, but can sustain contraction for much longer, both continuously and spasmodically. They are invested with a greater blood supply and use aerobic energy production (using oxygen, Fig. 5) to supply their needs. Again the final source of energy is ATP, but it is produced by lengthy biochemical processes involving the breakdown of sugars and fatty acids to the waste products carbon dioxide and water. These reactions are far more efficient in terms of producing ATP than are the anaerobic mechanisms, but they are much slower. This fits in with the pattern of slow but long-reacting red fibres. The ratio of sugars (mainly glucose) to fatty acids (produced from fats in the diet either direct or from fatty tissue around the body) depends on the availability of each. Other factors also influence what starting compound is used, such as how long the muscle action has lasted, how much adrenaline is circulating and whether caffeine has been taken close to exercise. Generally speaking, the sugars are more available than the fatty acids because glucose is produced by the chemically simple breakdown of glycogen (a complex carbohydrate polymer formed from glucose molecules joined together) stored actually in the muscle. This means that, until the glycogen is exhausted, glucose tends to be the main energy producer. However, both sources of raw material are vital for the production of energy within the muscles.

In both red and white fibres there are small, ovaloid particles, the function of which was long unclear. These were called mitochondria and are now known to be the power-stations of the cells. They contain all the necessary chemicals to produce ATP and the other compounds which comprise the energy production system. They are thus the centres of activity during muscle use. Their role and function within the cell have now been extensively explored and recently they have been found to be important not only in energy production but also in other major cell activities. Interestingly, they appear to have been separate entities that in the long distant past combined with other organisms in a symbiotic relationship.

## THE BLOOD AND NERVE SUPPLY

The blood supply to the muscles (Fig. 6) is simple. It consists of a main supply of oxygenated blood from the heart, carried through the arteries. These blood vessels then branch out to form a system of arterioles (smaller arteries within the muscle-connecting tissue). These in turn divide to form the capillaries (very small blood vessels) which have very thin walls to allow the exchange of gases, water and dissolved biochemicals (mainly sugars, amino acids, fatty acids, hormones, minerals and vitamins) between the blood and the muscle cells. The capillaries, having exchanged chemicals with the fluid surrounding the muscles (interstitial fluid), then rejoin to form venules (small veins) and finally veins that carry deoxygenated blood (which also contains waste products) back to the heart. The blood is then pumped to the lungs for reoxygenation, and is continually circulated through the liver, where waste products are removed or destroyed and vital chemicals added. The whole system is called the cardiovascular system.

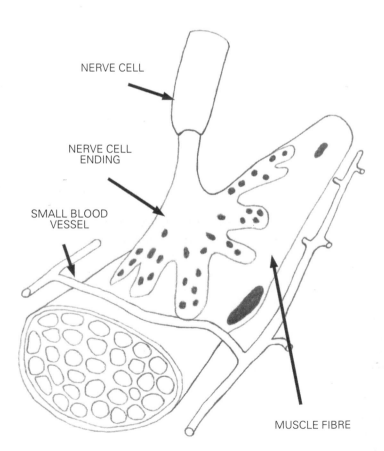

NERVE CELL

NERVE CELL ENDING

SMALL BLOOD VESSEL

MUSCLE FIBRE

Fig. 6 Nerve and muscle supply to a muscle fibre.

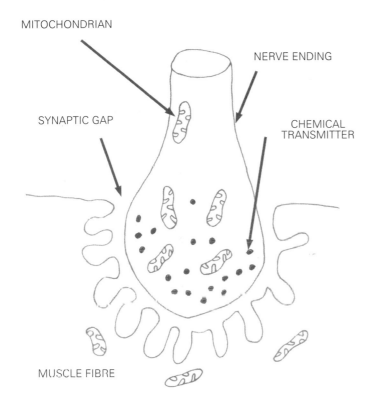

MITOCHONDRIAN

NERVE ENDING

SYNAPTIC GAP

CHEMICAL
TRANSMITTER

MUSCLE FIBRE

Fig. 7 A nerve ending.

The efficiency of this system determines, to a great extent, the aerobic fitness level of the athlete, and can be dramatically improved by training. One of the effects of training is to increase the size and the extent of the blood circulation within the muscle. This results in the trained muscle swelling more than the untrained during exercise.

The nerve supply to the muscles (Fig. 6) superficially appears similar to the blood system. It is different, however, in that each nerve going to a muscle is really a bundle of nerve cells, like an electrical cable. Each nerve cell has a cell body higher up in the nervous system and has its own connections up to the brain. This actually means that each nerve cell that ends at a muscle cell or group of muscle cells will behave slightly differently from all its neighbours. In terms of the result of maximal nervous stimulation, these differences are not significant, but they do allow very fine control over the extent and duration of muscle contractions at sub-maximal levels.

Each nerve running to a muscle tends to be closely associated with the blood vessels in its path through the connective tissue to the muscles. Each nerve cell ends attached direct to a muscle fibre via a chemical connection called a synapse. This looks like a bulb pushing into the muscle cell surface (Fig. 7). The gap between the nerve cell end and the muscle cell is called the synaptic gap and must be bridged if the nerve is to convey its message to the muscle. This is achieved by the release of chemicals (transmitters) when the nerve is stimulated. These have a specific action on the muscle cell membrane, changing its structure to allow minerals (sodium and potassium) to change sides rapidly across the membrane.

Simply put, the sodium goes into the muscle fibres and the potassium comes out. This influx of sodium causes an internal release of calcium that stimulates the ATP to break down, thus releasing the energy for contraction. The sodium remains as long as the nerve is being stimulated. After the cessation of nervous stimuli, the reverse action happens, with the potassium flowing in and the sodium flowing out. This stops the release of energy and thus the contraction. It is not necessary to know how all this happens, but it is important to understand that the minerals both in the muscle fibres themselves as well as in the interstitial fluid (water-like liquid surrounding all internal tissues) play a vital role in the whole contraction/relaxation process. This explains why a correct mineral balance in the body as a whole must be maintained at all costs if efficient muscular activity is required. The sodium and potassium are intimately involved with the nervous stimulation and the calcium with stabilizing the nerve and muscle cell membranes electrically and stimulating the release of energy from the ATP – any imbalance of these key chemicals disrupts the normal functioning of the muscle.

The whole system of nerves and muscles is called the neuro-muscular system. This and the cardiovascular system and the muscles themselves comprise the three major functional systems of voluntary (as well as involuntary) action within the human body. Therefore it is essential that in the training of athletes these be understood at least at a basic level, so that the reasons behind certain training and body maintenance methods may also be understood. Too frequently training techniques are adopted because someone says that they work, rather than their having any physiological basis. This is not to say that all methods need to be fully explained scientifically to have any value. For a particular job to be done there are very definite, correct ways to achieve it which have their basis in physiology rather than folklore.

# CHAPTER 3
# Strength – What Is It ?

The last chapter gave some insight into the structure and function of the muscles. We shall now try to use this information and extend it to an understanding of exactly what is meant by strength.

This question is the starting point for everyone who needs to develop in his or her sport, and it is normally given a wrong or at best an incomplete answer. This is because most people have their own understanding of the word and thus interpret the question only in relation to their own concept. To clarify the position we must first define 'strength' in all its different guises, and then relate it to our needs.

We often hear phrases like 'a strong shot putter' or 'a strong sprinter' or even 'a strong marathon runner', but obviously the strengths referred to mean different things in each context. There are many types of strength but they fall within the two main categories of static and dynamic strength. Static means non-moving and this type of strength is therefore the ability to apply force against a non-moving resistance; another word for static is isometric.

Dynamic strength is far more complex because there are many ways of moving and the type of strength involved must relate to the type of movement. The body can move quickly or slowly; the pattern and the speed of movement of the relevant body parts may vary; the body or parts of it may be accelerating or decelerating. These details must be examined to elucidate the several dynamic strengths involved in athletic motion. A better understanding of how these ideas relate to a movement can be gained only by a better knowledge of the major concepts.

Fig. 8 The strength of a jumper. (Mark Shearman)

## STATIC OR ISOMETRIC STRENGTH

This type of strength is of limited interest to the athlete. The fundamentals of all athletic movements require the levers to work dynamically, but, even so, certain areas of the body need to be fixed or held close to fixed positions during movements in order to maintain posture. The development of this static strength in the relevant regions can therefore benefit the overall core stability and athletic ability. Static strength has been studied in depth in many countries, but it has been used extensively only for bodybuilding, a sport in which coordinated movements are not required as a means of improving performance. Charles Atlas was the best-known exponent of static strength training in this regard, and, in fact, helped greatly to further the cause of strength training generally when it was found that his methods led to a performance decrease rather than an increase when applied to dynamic movements. The search for new methods was thus stimulated and the field of specific strength training opened up.

Now the use of static strength training is increasing in athletics and relates to the improvement of the postural muscle groups such as those of the back and the abdomen. The main problem with their more extensive

Fig. 9 The direction of force in a back squat.

| | | |
|---|---|---|
| *Slow dynamic* | i) | concentric – isotonic/isokinetic |
| | ii) | eccentric – isotonic/isokinetic |
| *Fast dynamic* | i) | concentric – isotonic/isokinetic/plyometric |
| | ii) | eccentric – isotonic/isokinetic |
| | iii) | plyometric. |

use revolves around the difficulty in strengthening the muscles throughout their whole range. If a simple squat movement (Fig. 9) is performed against an immovable resistance when the legs are flexed to 90 degrees, the result is an increase in strength over only a small angle (approximately 15 degrees) either side of the fixed position. This means that to strengthen the muscle throughout the full range of movement about six positions of fixed resistance must be used. This, of course, is not only very time-consuming but also boring in the extreme and leads to a rapid decrease in effectiveness. Nevertheless, such exercises may be used as a short-term change in routine to some effect. To summarize: static strength is of only limited importance to the athlete but can be used for specific purposes.

## DYNAMIC OR MOVING STRENGTH

There are many ways of moving either the whole or parts of the body during athletic activities. The types of strength involved in each way relate to the use of the different muscle fibres of the muscles. For example, we have seen that the white (fast) fibres are associated with rapid movements and that energy sources are different from the red (slow) fibres. Thus we may expect that the qualities of each fibre type will not only produce different strengths when operative

but also require different methods to enhance their strength. The different ways of moving must therefore be understood in order to define as clearly as possible the type of dynamic strength involved.

These ways of moving may be broadly categorized (*see* box above).

These terms need explanation so that it can be seen how they fit into the total pattern of strength training.

### Concentric and Eccentric Movements

These two terms refer to the direction of the movement. Concentric means the normal direction of motion produced during contraction of the muscle groups concerned, and eccentric means movement in the opposite direction (that is, during the relaxation or extension of the muscle groups). This is exemplified by the squat in which the legs are bent and then straightened. On the downward part of the exercise the muscles are working eccentrically to maintain the correct pattern of movement. When the upward path is started, the muscles are working concentrically to extend the legs. The significance of this is that work must obviously be done in both directions to complete the exercise. Thus both concentric and eccentric muscular exercise are performed. It has been found, however, that more resistance can be handled by the muscles eccentrically than concentrically.

This is related to the fact that eccentric movements are aided by gravity and thus have an assisting external force.

On the basis of this, strength-training exercises either work the concentric or the eccentric movement hard. Since the loadings taken differ to provide equal difficulty, they cannot be done to the same level of intensity during the same exercise. However, it is obvious that some gain is made in both directions of movement if they are controlled. This is one reason why resistance exercises are rarely performed at maximum speed eccentrically.

## Isotonic, Isokinetic and Plyometric Movements

These terms relate to the way in which the muscle works and broadly depend on how the resistance is applied or the movement executed during the exercise. Isotonic movements are those involving a constant resistance. Thus a barbell in a bench press will weigh the same throughout the exercise. Since the muscles' ability to apply force increases as the bar is pushed up, the movement is an accelerating one. All exercises against a constant resistance have

Figs 10 & 11 The back squat.

this characteristic; that is, in fact, the basic movement characteristic of the body parts.

In simple terms, the body part must be moved and is therefore accelerated. The force necessary to perform this function is applied by the muscles through the levers. Each part of the initial movement is made up of many coordinated contractions and relaxations in the muscles, each one starting and stopping at the appropriate time. Thus each part of the movement is itself made up of accelerating actions (as well as decelerations). At no time does any part of the body perform uniform speed movements during athletic movements conducted in air (swimming in water is different). Even when the body reaches a uniform speed during running, the individual parts of it that produce the movement are still speeding up and slowing down. From this it must be concluded that the essential nature of athletic movement is one of isotonic actions, a fact that must be taken into consideration when analysing a sport or event.

Isokinetic movements are those performed against a resistance that increases progressively through the range of movement. This increase is meant to vary according to the muscle's ability to apply force during its action. When this is so, the movement has a mainly non-accelerating characteristic that relates most closely to sports in which water provides resistance to motion. Movements in air encounter little resistance of this nature, and so far as strength-training methods go, isokinetics has more specific than general applications. There has been much research into the efficacy of such methods, some of which have relevance to the athlete, and seem to indicate that isokinetic exercises have value. The problems relate to whether the machines in service are truly isokinetic. With most of them this is not the case, simply because, to initiate the movement, acceleration must take place. Generally, after this initial phase even the simplest machines provide close approximations to uniform speed movements. The simple resistance pulley used by swimmers is effective, but the actual performance of the exercises meets the same problems as isometrics in that it is unmeasurable and boring as a result. Since even the most sophisticated isokinetic machines lack a good measuring device there is really no way of knowing whether there is any improvement. Because of this, isokinetics must play a relatively insignificant role in strength development for the athlete. It might also be true to say that it is of more relevance when training the slower fibres because of the difficulty of achieving really fast isokinetic movements, which by definition are non-accelerating. My own feeling is that, for conditioning the muscles for endurance and in preparation for more specific training, isokinetic methods might have most value.

Plyometric activities are often called elastic or springing work. Neither term amply describes these types of activity since they involve the basic stretch reflexes of the muscle, the elastic recoil of the tendons and muscles, and the conscious contraction of the muscles. Recent work has also implicated changes in the muscle bridges in this type of movement. Plyometrics involves the prior, rapid stretching of the muscle before contraction. Thus a squat jump can be done in one of two ways. First, to bend the legs steadily and then jump; this is not plyometric. Secondly, to dip sharply and respond as rapidly as possible; this is plyometric. It is essential during such exercises to bend the limb rapidly and respond even faster. If the movement is not at absolute maximum speed then the stretch reflexes will add nothing to the movement and it will not be plyometric. This is why plyometrics is listed only under fast dynamic strength.

Although the exact nature of this type of strength has to be defined more exactly, it does seem that the application of plyometric training methods results in significant improvements in athletic performance in many events. The most obvious of these is in the jumps, where the take-off is almost exclusively of the stretch–react nature. For example, in the Fosbury flop the take-off foot is planted with a slight flexion of the knee, which is then vigorously extended. The efficiency of this movement depends on the speed and the range of extension, which are maximal when the action is plyometric rather than slow and deliberate. This is similar for the long jump, the triple jump and the pole-vault take-off. The triple jump has the additional stress of three consecutive extensions and thus the plyometric strength involved needs to be greater.

It is interesting to note that, in certain events, the application of plyometric strength at the wrong time in the movement is actually counterproductive. Take the discus turn and throw for example: if the plyometric response is initiated when the athlete lands from the turn, the hips will not have time to face the direction of delivery. It is vital to analyse the athletic movement concerned before the assumption is made that plyometrics will necessarily be beneficial.

## GENERAL AND LOCAL STRENGTH ENDURANCE

General strength endurance is the quality most sought after by runners. It is the ability to move a resistance, which may only be the body weight, for prolonged periods. Any activity lasting longer than 10 to 15sec requires this, since the immediate energy production takes place in the muscles. It is therefore true to say that strength endurance is actually more related to the energy-production systems and the efficiency of the

cardiovascular system than it is to actual strength. Nevertheless, resistance work may be done usefully in the gym to enhance the metabolic and physical processes within the muscles. This is accomplished by working the whole body either against gravity or some other light resistance. Alternatively, training individual muscle groups locally, to cover all those involved in the activity, can also be of benefit. It is best to combine local and general exercises. This gives the greatest increase in efficiency.

Local strength endurance is that ability to perform prolonged work against resistance in a very localized area of the body. For example, the legs can be made to work much harder during the last phase of a sprint if local strength endurance is worked on. In addition, the conditioning phase in the athletes' training programme can be made most effective if some local muscular endurance work is included. Obviously the balance of general and specific work depends on the sport and the event.

The three main areas of improvement come from increased vascularity of the muscles, improved metabolic efficiency at cellular level, and improved metabolic efficiency outside the cell. These three factors relate to both the aerobic and the anaerobic efficiency of the muscle, which are the qualities most essential for running events up to and beyond the marathon.

## SPORT AND EVENT ANALYSIS

To perform the task of analysing the types of strength and the relative quantities used in a sport or an event, it is first necessary to ask and answer the question, 'What movements are involved?' This is not as easy as one might expect. Let us take the example of the 100m sprint.

This event consists of the start, the acceleration phase, the maintenance phase and the speed-endurance phase. Each of

Fig. 12 The sprint start – 'On your marks'. (Dan Grossman)

Fig. 13 The sprint start – 'Get set'. (Dan Grossman)

Fig. 14 The drive from the blocks. (Dan Grossman)

these requires different uses of the muscles and thus must be treated separately. The start itself has three parts: the relaxed, initial position (Fig. 12), the static 'set' position (Fig. 13), and the actual drive into the start itself (Fig. 14). Each of these requires a different set of abilities. The initial part requires little in the way of physical activity and generally needs relaxation and the minimum of energy consumption. The 'set' position is effectively static, requiring considerable strength from the shoulders to the fingers. This means that specific static strength in these areas is of importance. The actual start or drive is accomplished mainly through extending the legs, with the body weight as resistance. This means that the movement is largely isotonic, although there is a stretch of the Achilles tendon immediately before the drive, thus making the initial movement plyometric. This is not necessarily an advantage if a smoother, less energy-consuming start is required, as in the 400m. During the start, the back and the abdominal muscles are maintaining the posture of the body and are thus working isometrically.

The acceleration phase of the run involves the legs driving behind the centre of gravity. The quadriceps are therefore working in the isotonic mode, as are the arms, although the latter have no resistance to their action apart from their own weight. As the body becomes erect, the hamstrings and gluteus muscle groups come more into play, and again they work isotonically. This brings the athlete into the speed maintenance phase, when relaxation is so important to minimize energy consumption. The muscles, however, are still working as they do at the end of the acceleration phase. As this phase proceeds, the immediate energy sources start to run out and the athlete enters the phase of speed endurance. The muscles are then working with diminishing anaerobic resources and therefore need strength endurance to continue effective force application. From this analysis it can be seen that, even with such an apparently simple event, all types of strength are involved in one way or another. The strength programme therefore needs to take all of this into consideration.

## SUMMARY

The table below summarizes the information in graphic form, showing the interrelationships between all the different types of strength. It is most important that the athlete and the coach should be aware of the nature of these, in order to make the correct analysis of the event. So often a lack of understanding leads to bad results, with the incorrect conclusion being drawn that strength training is useless for a particular sport, event or person. If the correct analysis is made then the results will be good.

The varied types of strength also give us some insight into the complexity of training. It is not essential to use complex terminology to define what are in essence simple concepts. The fundamental requirements for strength training are: a knowledge of how the muscles work; a knowledge of the various types of strength and how they relate to each sport or event; and the ability to plan a programme using the available and relevant strength techniques.

The first two of these have now been covered. The last is the basis for the following chapters and will relate the information gained so far to the practical aspects of training and the further development of these themes.

## Types of strength

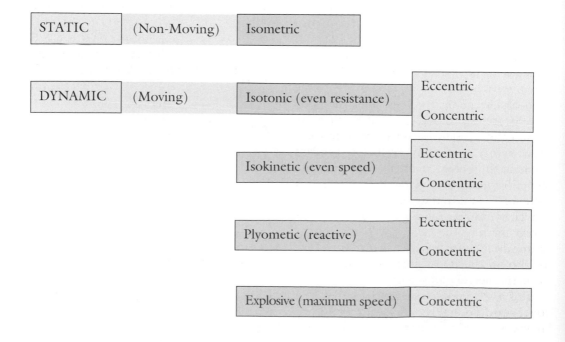

# CHAPTER 4

# Planning a Programme for the Year

The term 'training programme' covers a multitude of diverse action plans, some of which often prove to be extremely effective while others are purely counterproductive. Strength work must be integrated into the full programme of training. These programmes are normally set for a period of one year so that any modification is more easily implemented. Some coaches attempt to plan for major games cycles such as that of the four-yearly Olympics. This, however, can never be set in concrete as the unexpected always happens and some modification will be needed.

Most of the work done on developing detailed training programmes was carried out in the former USSR and East Germany over the thirty years before the fall of the Berlin Wall, and, despite their different social systems, much of the work still has relevance. The programming of training is now the rule rather than the exception. The main obstacle to introducing such ideas was that Western training tended to be very empirically oriented, the 'old traditional' ideas being considered the best. In this instance, however, science has overtaken mythology and the new ideas are based on solid research and development, in the practical as well as the theoretical environment. In addition to the difficulties of implementing such programming, there has also been a lack of simple texts to explain the ideas concisely and clearly.

This chapter is designed to assist the coach and the athlete to expand their knowledge of the subject. It is divided into two parts: introducing the basic methodology and terminology of strength training, and the planning of a year's programme.

## THE BASIC METHODOLOGY AND TERMINOLOGY OF STRENGTH TRAINING

The fundamental principle of strength gain is that of progressively increasing difficulty (resistance, in most instances) during the training period. Many athletes have injured themselves in strength training, but this is usually due to a lack of understanding of the methods or of their own physiology when attempting to progress. In most instances such injuries can in the main be avoided. Safety during strength training is the starting point for all beginners, and the gospel from then on. Full attention must be paid right from the outset in order to ingrain the correct sense of discipline, which is essential for the safe development of strength.

### Safety in the Gymnasium

Safety starts with the attitude of the athlete to his or her training. It is totally pointless, and often dangerous, even to start such work, without a serious and positive attitude to learning the correct methods. Often athletes train in the gym laughing and joking in mid session. Nine times out of ten nothing happens, but the tenth time someone gets injured and a promising career is terminated prematurely. Total concentration must be applied throughout the work. To help in developing the correct attitude the coach must explain to the athletes what can go wrong if full concentration is not applied.

To help to ensure safety within the gym, certain additional equipment will be needed:

1. A good pair of tightly fitting, flat-soled trainers and, ideally, a pair of lifting boots or at least solid, flat-soled work boots for the athletes lifting heavy weights;
2. Warm but not baggy clothing to prevent cooling down during training;
3. A good, stiff, weight-training belt (4in wide at the back, 2in at the front) to help support the mid region during certain exercises;
4. Some magnesium carbonate powder (gymnastic 'chalk') to keep the hands dry; this gives an excellent grip on the bar.

These are the minimum requirements and additional items, such as a lifting leotard, wrist wraps and straps to aid in gripping the bar, are normally needed only by more advanced trainers.

### Injuries

Most injuries occur because of incorrect technique, either through a lack of knowledge or ill-discipline. This inability to perform the exercises correctly makes the lifting of heavy weights dangerous. The exercises used in strength training are in the main easy to perform and have little danger involved in them. However, certain vital exercises need specific positions to be used or held. If this is not done, some part of the body comes under undue strain and may be injured. This mainly applies to exercises involving the legs, the shoulders and the back.

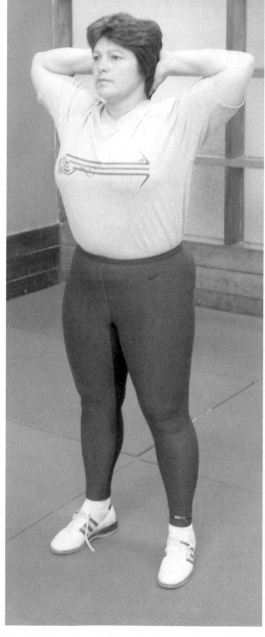

Fig. 15 Suitable clothing is essential.

Taking the back squat as an example will help to explain this point. This exercise is essentially simple to perform. The legs are bent and then straightened; if no resistance is applied and the movement is performed slowly, it does not matter too much in what position the back and the head are. However, to increase strength, resistance is usually applied by putting a resistance in the form of a barbell on the shoulders. This means that the legs are applying the power through the back to the shoulders in order to lift the weight. Unless the back is held straight and firm this force cannot be directly, effectively and safely transmitted. The back may round, straining the muscles of that region, or the weight may roll forward on to the neck with obvious dangers. Therefore during squatting it is essential to start with and maintain a straight and firm back.

## Mobility and Suppleness

Surprisingly, many athletes find this simple squatting movement hard to do correctly, usually due to a lack of mobility in the ankles or the length of the Achilles tendon. This is why it is recommended that a period of at least one month is needed to learn the basic movements before any resistance above 10 or 20kg is used. In some instances longer is required, particularly if the athlete has a serious lack of joint mobility or muscle-tendon suppleness. This quite often applies to the endurance runners who tend to neglect even the most basic mobility and suppling work in their training. Many such athletes have difficulty in touching their toes, or crouching with head up and heels on the ground. It is strongly advised that, if the athlete has this sort of problem, a period of general mobility and suppling is undertaken before strength training is begun. The problem of a lack of suppleness often occurs in younger athletes usually as a result of rapid bone growth. Care must be taken in this situation not to put undue

stress on the athlete as this can lead to physical damage to the growing areas of the bone.

The best results are gained by making sure that the correct tuition is given from the earliest age. A process of both physical and technical education usually guarantees that at least the athlete understands what he or she should be doing, even if it takes many months to achieve. If strength training is approached in this way, then the risks should be minimal.

## The Correct Pattern of Development

The young athlete and the older beginner must start in the same way, which is to train the body in the most complete way possible *without additional resistance*, to ensure that it has the strength and mobility to handle most movements. This is accomplished by performing a period of body-weight training which involves the athlete in using the body-weight as the resistance for the exercises. There are many ways of doing this, but the best results are achieved by combining major muscle group development with coordinated, general training.

Progress is achieved by increasing the number of times each exercise is repeated (repetitions). For the best results, exercises are performed within a formalized structure (session). This can be accomplished by using the same basic formula for session design as you would for weight or heavy resistance training. This will be discussed in detail in Chapter 5.

Following on from this body-weight training there should be a lengthy period of technical education, to teach the fundamental movement patterns for the major exercises that are going to be used in the programme. To do this a very light resistance is used; even the weakest and worst athletes can handle a 10kg bar comfortably. It is essential that the

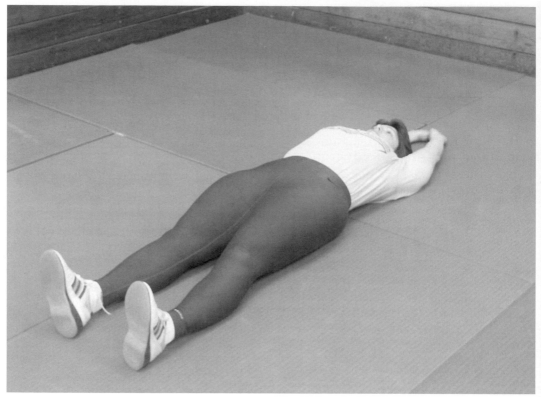

Fig. 16 Body-weight training.

techniques of each exercise are taught thoroughly and no compromise should be accepted at this stage. It is either right or wrong and the athlete must realize that future development depends on learning the correct way to perform the required movements. It is all too easy to accept partially correct positions, but the temptation should be resisted for the sake of safety and later success.

When these first two stages of training have been successfully accomplished, only then should increased resistance be applied during the exercise. The length of time before this stage is reached will vary considerably and depend on the initial fitness of the athlete. Some people naturally learn skills faster than others and it is thus the responsibility of the coach to ensure that each athlete receives individual training in the early stages.

The first three-month training period for the beginner would therefore be spent as shown in the table below.

| *Month 1* | *Month 2* | *Month 3* |
|---|---|---|
| body-weight training | technique | low-level resistance work |

| *Month 1* | *Month 2 and 3* | *Month 4* |
|---|---|---|
| body-weight training | heavy strength training | specific training |

This early training will set the general pattern for the later and more advanced programmes which essentially follow a similar structure. However, the technique learning phase is omitted and a period of specific training included. This relates directly to the sport or event in both exercise content and attitude. A four-month programme might therefore look like that shown in the box above for the more advanced trainer.

For most athletes, training for any longer than eight weeks on the same session becomes counterproductive, and so each period should not exceed this span without change. If a longer period is required, the best way to maintain progress is to break it into two sub-periods each performing the same task but in different ways. For example, a four-month strength period could be designed by constructing two separate schedules in which the majority of the exercises are different, but the emphasis on the muscle groups to be trained is the same.

To summarize this, the beginner follows a three-stage cycle of work (each stage lasting from four to six weeks):

body-weight training (conditioning)

technique weight training (education)

increasing resistance weight training (strength)

Fig. 17 Increasing resistance weight training.

Fig. 18 Specific strength training.

When the athlete is considered technically and physically competent (in six months to one year), a more advanced programme can be followed (each period again lasting from four to six weeks):

> body-weight training and some light weight training (conditioning)
>
> increasing resistance weight training (strength)
>
> specific strength training with weighted equipment (event related)

As the athlete develops within his or her event it becomes more essential to relate each period to a relevant time of year so that the specific work coincides with a competitive peak. This is the foundation of training planning (periodization).

## THE YEAR PLAN

For most athletes the simplest way of planning the year relates to defining the competition periods. In general, middle- and long-distance runners tend to adopt a double periodized year (two training cycles) and the explosive events a triple periodized year (three training cycles). However, the essential planning for both is similar.

The plan may be visualized by setting out a simple paper graph showing the twelve months. First the competitions are marked, second the starting date for the year is selected and a conditioning phase of four (triple periodized year) to eight weeks (double periodized year) marked down.

The specific (or peak competition) phases are then marked in to cover a run up to the first competition of around three weeks and extending over all the competitions themselves. Remember that these phases should be no longer than eight weeks for the best results. The double year would have a peak in the winter (cross-country or road races) and then another in the summer (track season). The triple year would have one in the winter (probably for indoor competition), one in early summer (early and mid-season competitions) and then another in late summer (for major championships). These peaks must reflect the competition aims of the athlete and can be adjusted accordingly. This then leaves us with gaps in the plan, where the general strength training is performed.

The phase lengths can be variable and sometimes, if there are only a few weeks

**A simple year plan**

|              | Sep  | Oct  | Nov  | Dec  | Jan  | Feb   | Mar  | Apr  | May  | Jun  | Jul  | Aug  | Sep  |
|--------------|------|------|------|------|------|-------|------|------|------|------|------|------|------|
| competition  |      | ---- | ---- | ---x | --x- | -x-x- | ---- | ---- | --xx | x-x- | x--- | ---x | x--- |
| period       |      | 1    | 1    | 1    | 1    | 1     | 2    | 2    | 2    | 2    | 2    | 3    | 3    |
| conditioning | rest | xxxx |      |      |      |       |      |      |      |      |      |      |      |
| strength     |      |      | xxxx | xxxx |      |       | xxxx | xxxx |      |      |      |      |      |
| specific     |      |      |      |      | xxxx | xxxx  |      | xxxx | xxxx |      | xxxx | xxxx |      |
| intermediate |      |      |      |      |      |       |      |      |      | xxxx |      |      |      |

between peaks, it is wise to create a different phase style to reflect the correction of problems found in earlier peaks. These are usually called intermediate phases.

A typical double periodized year might look like as in the table above.

The skill in constructing the programme is achieving the right balance between training and competition. Every athlete is unique and it might be impossible to get it right until after you have known the athlete a while and understand how he or she reacts to your training plan. Bearing this in mind, never be worried about seeking feedback from the athletes and changing the year plan according to their responses and perceived needs.

It is a good idea to introduce even the younger athletes to the discipline of year planning. You will find out from the application of such a plan which of them are committed to serious training and can cope with a structured format for training.

### Structure of Training Periods

For the beginner, two sessions of strength training per week are adequate, and each should last from about 60 to 90min. For the more advanced athlete this would be two to three sessions per week, and can be up to five sessions for the international class athlete in the heavy throwing events.

The exercises within each session are laid down in a carefully structured way, which will be discussed in Chapter 6. The regular pattern of exercises within the sessions and the way in which progress is made (increased repetitions or resistance) for the particular period is called a schedule. Thus we might have a conditioning schedule, a technique schedule and a strength schedule for the beginner. For the more advanced athlete we would have a conditioning schedule, a strength schedule and a specific schedule.

The number of exercises in each session within the schedule depends on its purpose but follows the guidelines below:

| conditioning | 10–15 exercises |
|--------------|-----------------|
| technique    | 6–10 exercises  |
| strength     | 5–8 exercises   |
| specific     | 5–8 exercises   |

### Sets and Repetitions

A set is the term used for a group of repetitions (single performances of a movement). Thus a set of any exercise could contain from one performance to a hundred (or more) repetitions. It is usual to include between four and twelve sets of each exercise in a session. For strength gain, these sets are performed consecutively and not one set of one exercise followed by one set of another, as in circuit training. The reason for this is that the muscle group gets progressively more tired and more effort must be applied to perform the exercise, bringing in more fibres as the sets progress; this is called stage training.

In a circuit, the exercise is performed only once every cycle and thus there is more time in which to recover than in stage training, the effect therefore being more general.

*The number of sets and repetitions determines the effect of the session and is probably the most crucial aspect in designing the schedule.*

• A low number of sets containing a high number of repetitions increases local or general muscular endurance and can be performed only with little or no resistance (for example, four sets of fifty). The recovery between sets should be from 20 to 60sec.

• A medium number of sets containing a medium number of repetitions (for example, six sets of ten) with a medium-level resistance (with from 30 to 90sec recovery), increases strength to some degree but also bulks the muscles and increases strength endurance.

If the resistance is low and the exercises are performed at maximum speed (with from 10 to 30sec recovery), power will be the main effect. The importance of the speed of movement when performing resistance exercises will be discussed later.

• A high number of sets containing a low number of repetitions increases strength maximally (for example, ten sets of two). Such training is performed with near maximum resistance and should not be attempted by beginners. The rest between sets should be long enough for full recovery, probably around 2 to 4min.

To summarize: the higher the number of repetitions, the greater the endurance effect; the lower the number, the greater the strength effect.

## The Speed Factor

The speed at which an exercise is performed is of great importance to the athlete. Given the structure of muscle, with its two main types of fibre (fast and slow), it is vital to make sure that the speed of movement is not ignored. Even for the long-distance events the fast fibres are of great significance, particularly in view of the way in which most top quality races are run and won, with a very fast finish. It is clear from recent research that the faster the exercise is performed, the greater is the effect on fast fibres. Therefore this must be taken into consideration when planning the schedules.

A major mistake made in the early development of strength training was that it was thought that, if you performed slow, heavy exercises for a period, the strength gained could then be converted into fast strength by a period of fast exercises. This seems to be untrue, and it is now accepted that if you want to train the fast muscle fibres, everything must be done very fast, or at the least some fast exercises must be included in the schedule.

This becomes a problem only for the strength-based athletes, particularly in the throws, when maximum strength gain leads to a slow bias in the schedules; it is then necessary to ensure that the schedules are balanced as far as possible to improve the explosive power of the fast fibres. This is helped as much by the state of mind during the sessions as anything else. If the athlete attempts to perform the exercises as fast as possible, even when using a heavy weight, then the results will be far better than the slow, heavy grinds performed by most power-lifters (the sport for slow, strong people in which three exercises are performed for the sheer strength with speed being irrelevant).

This is another reason for starting beginners on very light resistance, since it is far easier to perform the exercises rapidly, thus stimulating the fast fibres in preference to the slow.

Fig. 19 Speed shown in power snatch.

The slow performance of exercises can in certain circumstances be useful. In the extreme, sets of an exercise performed at the rate of ten to twelve repetitions per minute with a light weight is a way of working the muscles very hard without putting a heavy resistance on them. This can be used to maintain leg strength during leg or back injuries when only light weights are possible. However, such methods are best used in conjunction with fast exercises.

## Plyometric Exercises

For the jumping events particularly, plyometric strength is a vital ingredient of the programme. Improvement in plyometric strength is determined by the way the exercises are performed. This difference was mentioned in Chapter 3, and it should be emphasized here that great benefit can be gained from the performance of exercises in a plyometric way, as long as the movements used relate to the event. In fact, such activities are far easier to control in the gym than at the track. Jumpers can usefully work on plyometrics with weights as well as by depth jumping and bounding.

One reason for performing gym plyometrics is that depth jumping is probably the most dangerous of all activities attempted in modern training. It is highly effective, but many athletes have been injured in the process of depth jumping and bounding. Most of the danger occurs when improvement is sought by raising the height of the box used to jump from or of the hurdles for bounding over. This is not so much of a problem in weight plyometrics, because the resistance can be increased carefully and accurately, depending on the ability of the athlete. In addition, the number and types of exercise can be carefully controlled to avoid injuries and yet still be effective.

The basic set and repetition structures discussed already often become limiting for

Figs 20–22 Plyometric bench squat jumps.

the athlete who must train heavily for strength. To this end many different structures have been devised and tried in the search for quicker and more effective results. These novel and challenging systems are also of use in overcoming the problem of periods of non-improvement, which plague the serious strength trainer.

### Advanced Set and Repetition Structures

*Pyramids*

The pyramid or half pyramid structure is probably the most popular of all of these. This entails the performance of an exercise in such a way that the repetitions decrease and the resistance increases, followed by the reverse. For example:

set 1: 8 repetitions with 50kg
set 2: 6 repetitions with 60kg
set 3: 4 repetitions with 70kg
set 4: 3 repetitions with 75kg
set 5: 2 repetitions with 80kg
set 6: 2 repetitions with 85kg
        and vice versa

A half pyramid, like that above, is the most often used, and the second half in which the repetitions increase and the weight drops is seldom used. This system may be applied to find the maximum possible strength by including several singles at the end, but this must be tried only by the more experienced athlete. The most important use of the pyramid system is to cover all aspects of strength gain (with the exception of long-term endurance) in one go. Thus the higher repetition/lower resistance sets work on muscular endurance, muscle size and strength, and the lower repetition/higher resistance sets emphasize strength gain.

## Bi- and Tri-Sets

Sometimes it is useful to work specific groups of muscles harder than can be done with the normal setting structure. The bi- and tri-set system is one way to do this. This involves the use of two or three exercises for muscles in a group, done consecutively with no break. For example, leg extension and leg biceps curl. One bi-set of this consists of a set of each exercise performed with no break. A tri-set for the shoulders could be made up of flying exercise, lateral raise and bent-over rowing, one set of each constituting the tri-set. It is usual to perform up to four bi- or tri-sets, since they are very tiring, as a session. They can also be performed with very little recovery between each bi- or tri-set, but in this instance a lighter resistance or lower repetitions need to be used.

## Super-Sets

The same principle can be applied to a single muscle, in which instance the set is called a super-set. Combining two or three exercises for the same muscle is an effective way of making rapid gains in bulk and strength. An example for the triceps could be a super-set made up of narrow-grip bench press, standing triceps press and triceps push down. Performed as individual super-sets this is hard enough, but when four to six cycles are performed continuously it becomes exceedingly demanding. These combination sets are best performed after any high quality work has been done – since they completely exhaust the muscles.

## Pre-Exhaustion

In view of the fact that there are two types of fibre in the muscles, a theory has been put forward that they can be worked most effectively if one or the other is pre-exhausted. This has led to the concept of pre-exhaustion in strength training. It is said that, if you use a light weight and perform a set of an exercise to exhaustion and then follow this by several heavier sets with fewer repetitions, then in the latter stage you will train mainly the fast fibres. If the process is reversed by hitting maximum resistance to exhaustion and then performing light high-repetition sets, then the slow fibres are said to be worked predominantly. However, it is not clear whether this works in such a way because of the complex mechanism for the recruitment of the fibres in any muscular activity. Nevertheless, pre-exhaustion seems to be effective in promoting strength gains.

Figs 23–26 Bi-set of standing biceps curl and standing triceps press.

*Burn-Downs*

Figs 27&28 Start of first and last sets of a burn-down standing biceps curl, showing the initial use of a number of small weights.

When the muscles are worked continuously, they become fatigued and are able to apply less and less force. At this stage, as many fibres that are available are being used. This factor has been exploited in the use of burn-downs. As the name suggests, these are very hard and painful to do, but again are effective in working the muscle hard. They consist of one exercise performed in the following way. A resistance is used which the athlete can perform for ten repetitions. One set of eight repetitions is then completed, at which stage the resistance is slightly reduced (by 5 to 10 per cent) and a further set performed with as little rest as it takes to change the weights. This is repeated six or eight times, with the resistance being reduced each set, at the end of which the muscle is usually completely exhausted.

For example, a biceps curl burn-down might be performed as follows:

| | |
|---|---|
| 1 · 8 | 50kg |
| 1 · 8 | 47.5kg |
| 1 · 8 | 45kg |
| 1 · 8 | 42.5kg |
| 1 · 8 | 40kg |
| 1 · 8 | 35kg |

This method is normally used with specific muscle-group exercises, such as arm biceps curl, rather than the multiple-action exercises such as the clean or snatch. Such routines are useful in increasing the strength of specific weak muscles, when they are limiting more complex movements or need to be rehabilitated after injury.

There are many more fiendish ways of getting muscles to increase in strength and it should now be clear that, with imagination, strength training can be kept interesting and continuously varied. The main problems come when the athlete ceases to show progress, and it is hoped that the ideas discussed so far show how this sort of problem can be resolved. There are many ways of doing this, but what gives the best results is to combine major muscle-group development with other, more specific muscular work.

# CHAPTER 5
# Strength Training for Running Events

## INTRODUCTION

From the previous chapters we have seen that the actual designing of a strength schedule is quite a complex task that cannot be attempted without sufficient knowledge. So far, it has been stressed that, for maximum results, it is vital that the event for which the schedule is required is analysed properly. Brief examples have been discussed, but now we shall look in more detail at what each event requires.

It is clear that this analysis must be considered in relation to the individual's requirements, but the general concepts behind analysing the event must be adhered to specifically, with the emphasis being put on the weak areas of that person's body. For example, we might find that a sprinter has particularly weak quadriceps. His or her schedule would take this into consideration by adding some extra exercises for those muscles to the basic routine rather than by changing the pattern of the routine.

It must be stressed that the analyses here are a matter of interpreting basic data. This means that there are several ways of looking

Fig. 29 Flat out in the sprints. (Dan Grossman)

at the events and mine is just one, albeit one based on considerable practical experience in the strength training of many athletes.

## THE RUNNING EVENTS

The analysis of running events, the subject of this chapter, seems, at first sight, one of singular ease. What, after all, could be easier than gaining strength to put one foot in front of the other? This, of course, is totally untrue and, in actuality, the subtleties of working out the schedules for each of the events makes these analyses the least easy. The psychological problems relating to track training make strength work for the runner one area where the programme can be made more interesting. Unfortunately, there are often problems getting runners to see the significance of strength training because the tradition has always been to work on running alone. However, the new generation of coaches and athletes has a far better knowledge of the workings of the body and of the training necessary to extract everything possible.

The groups of events for the sake of this résumé will be considered as follows: sprints and hurdles; middle distance; and long-distance and marathon. It must be said that all the events have the same basis of strength, although obviously the sprints have the added difficulty of the dynamic start; the sprints, then, will be discussed first.

## SPRINTS

### Conditioning

The sprints are events which require the most careful balancing of all the facets in each event. For example, it is considered that the short sprints are up to 95 per cent anaerobic muscle activity. However, in order to train sufficiently hard to gain increases in this anaerobic ability and the technique of sprinting, it is vital to include a significant level of aerobic work. Thus the initial conditioning phase of the programme must take this into consideration, and the strength work in the gym at this stage must also reflect the aerobic fitness required. This can be effected by making sure that the gym work is based on high repetitions with little rest in between each set.

The exercises included must reflect the events as far as possible. All the sprints revolve around the four phases:

> 1. The start
> 2. The acceleration
> 3. The maintenance phase.

Each phase requires the emphasis of a particular muscle group.

### 1. The Start

This is the most energy-consuming part of the activity and therefore considerable strength in the relevant muscles will facilitate energy conservation. The start itself has three parts: (a) the relaxed initial position; (b) the isometric 'set' position; and (c) the actual start or drive into the run. Obviously the initial position does not require any significant strength, but the second, isometric phase has a high static-strength content. The muscles involved include all the major muscle groups, the calves, legs, mid-region, shoulders and arms. Thus we must consider that some isometric activities must be included in the schedule, but probably not until the actual strength phase, although some indirect work can be done with certain exercises for the mid-region during the conditioning schedule.

Fig. 30 Powering out of the blocks. (Dan Grossman)

Of most significance are the muscles used in the actual start or drive, because these are significantly different from those used later on when the body becomes erect. By this I mean that, when the athlete initiates the drive from a crouch start, his centre of gravity is well in front of the point of contact with the ground, the toes. Later in the run this distance is dramatically reduced with a consequent change in the muscles required to actuate movement. This is perhaps the most critical area in the sprint, because if either is emphasized too much to the detriment of the other, then an incomplete sprinter will result.

The actual start, then, requires considerable power to take the strain not only of driving forward but also raising the body to a near vertical position. The amount of quadriceps strength needed depends on the spacing of the feet in the initial position. The position an athlete adopts is usually related to the strength and often you will see weak sprinters with close feet and a high hip position. This is because they do not have sufficient strength to drive from a position of tight knee bend. This can be remedied simply by strength training. The usual cause is that most coaches cannot see the reason for working the legs over a sufficient knee-bend range to allow the athlete to adopt the most efficient drive out position for him or her. This knee-bend range can only be extended by doing exercises beyond the required range, and in the conditioning phase such work as full knee-bend jumping or squatting with little or no weight (maximum 15kg) can bring miraculous results. These jumping activities are not to be performed plyometrically but should be done smoothly and with good balance for maximum effectiveness. It is certain that, if an athlete can perform four sets of thirty full squat jumps, then there is sufficient strength endurance over the full range of the muscles' action to start working on a lower hip position in the start. An additional advantage is also gained from these jumping activities, and this is that the whole lower body is used in a coordinated fashion. The quadriceps do most of the work, but the back, gluteus group, hamstrings, adductors and calves all put in sufficient work to be effectively improved. The conditioning, of course, will only improve the ability to work and not actually strengthen them much except in the weakest of individuals. But it does allow for strength phase work to be done in order to build the muscles later.

Another problem in the start is that of weak arms and shoulders, so that the athlete cannot hold a powerful lean forward in the 'set' position. Some sprinters will say that this is not important, but it is significant that the further forward you can lean, the more forward momentum will be present when the arm support is removed, thus giving a useful emphasis to the leg action. Arm and shoulder conditioning exercises are therefore vital in the schedule and can include such activities as press-ups of various forms, bench dips (good, rangy exercise), chins and/or supported chins and various arm movement exercises with very light resistance. In addition, exercises such as squat thrusts, burpees (squat thrust followed by a star jump) and sprint thrusts (similar to squat thrusts but bringing only one leg forward at a time to obtain the maximum separation between the legs) all use the arms isometrically and therefore have significance in enhancing the areas of strength needed in the start. All-round conditioning and strengthening of the shoulders is considered vital by most modern sprint coaches.

The mid-region is easily worked on, and, apart from during the early stages, should include rotational exercises. For example, sit-ups or back hyperextensions should include a twist during the movement and leg raises

need not only be straight. The reason for this is that, when running, considerable rotational strength is needed in the mid-region to gain the maximum range of movement with the legs. Often sprinters are guilty of working the stomach and the back in the one plane of movement, with the result that back and hamstring injuries develop with no apparent cause. The problem, of course, is that the rotational mid-region muscles are weak and unable to support the back during running.

## 2. The Acceleration

This phase of the sprint is the most crucial in attaining speed. It involves the powerful use of the whole legs from the hips to the toes. The muscles used are predominantly the quadriceps, although as the athlete becomes more erect bodily, then the emphasis moves on to the hamstrings and the calves. This is because the initial drive is exactly that, a drive. When the athlete is near-vertical the action is nearer a pull because the lead foot lands in front of the centre of gravity and the hips must therefore be moved forwards with the aid of the gluteus and the hamstring muscles. This changeover of priority muscle groups in this acceleration phase of the sprint may well be the cause of hamstring pulls and needs careful attention during strength training.

We have seen that most of the muscle groups have been covered by the exercises needed to enhance the start, but, additionally, the acceleration needs extra emphasis on the gluteus and the hamstring muscles. This can be effected by the use of single and double leg back-arching exercises as well as the various forms of split feet-position jumping and lunges, together with pulley work. These exercises are probably the most effective in the conditioning necessary to enhance overall bodily strength and increase the efficiency of the sprinter in the acceleration phase.

For the hurdles there is the added complication of the barriers that interrupt the smooth acceleration of the sprint. Clearly specific strength and skill training are required for such athletes to surmount these obstacles at the same time as attempting to accelerate to maximum speed. Exercises that specifically help are those for the hip-flexor, the mid-region rotational muscles and the calves, each of which comes under intense pressure during the events.

### 3. The Maintenance Phase

This phase of the sprint has more to do with local muscular endurance than strength, and it is therefore essential that the conditioning work reflects this factor. The exercise patterns discussed above relate to the specific muscles needed to sprint, but how these exercises are performed relates to the part of the race being run. When the short-term, anaerobic energy stores are becoming depleted, strength endurance comes into play. It is my feeling that all the gym work should contain a long-term, anaerobic element, even during the strength-gain phase. This is because the energy cycles can be improved dramatically, but they can also get worse very quickly if not maintained. The body is an endlessly adaptable machine and, when stress is put upon it, it responds by increasing adaptation to compensate. It is obvious therefore that should the stress be reduced, so will the body's response.

The method to adopt for the conditioning work is fairly simple: a minimum of two body-weight stage training sessions per week, with a possible third circuit-based session. The difference is that, during body-weight stage training, the exercises are completed individually before the next is attempted. This ensures that

maximum work is performed on the muscle group involved, without allowing it to recover fully, thus enhancing the anaerobic responses. In the circuit method, each exercise is performed in sequence, so that the muscle can rest before it is used again. This tends to make circuits more aerobic than anaerobic. Since sprinting is essentially anaerobic, body-weights seem the best way of training in the gym, but as we have already said, some aerobic work can effectively be added to the sprinters schedule.

The body-weights sessions are usually made up of low set/high repetition regimens, such as ten exercises, four sets of from ten to fifty repetitions. The total length of each session is between 30 and 60min, with fixed recoveries between sets and exercises (for example, 30sec between sets and 45sec between exercises). This means that improvements can be made by increasing the speed of exercises performed, although it should be stressed that technique and range of movement should not be sacrificed for speed.

## Strength

The conditioning schedule for the sprints contains all the essential ingredients for the strength-phase schedule, except, of course, that the emphasis must be altered to increase actual strength rather than exclusively strength endurance. This change of emphasis must be conducted without losing the gains made from the conditioning. This is effected by making sure that each session has some element of endurance involved.

The muscle groups that need to be strengthened are the same as those we have discussed above. The exercises used to make absolute strength gains should, I feel, be split up into the general as well as the specific, because the sprints use the whole body in a very balanced way. It is often said

Figs 31–35 Inclined twisting sit-ups for mid-region strength.

that the sprinter needs to be the complete athlete, although this is not strictly true since most of the work is done by the legs.

Basic exercises to include are those that work the legs, the mid-region and the arms in a coordinated fashion. In the repertoire of the strength trainer the best exercises overall are the power clean and the power snatch. These work the whole body in coordination and are simple to execute. They are also good exercises in which to lift fairly heavy weights, because they are self-limiting in

Figs 36&37 Bench sprint drives.

that, when the weight is too heavy, little damage can result from failure (assuming that the technique has been well taught). The split version of these exercises is of additional use because of the split-leg position that relates to the sprint action. The basic bench press is also a good general exercise in that it strengthens the whole chest, shoulder and arm region. It is, however, important not to get too involved in extensive bench pressing since the arm action in sprinting is not double. Therefore alternate dumb-bell bench or standing press would be a more effective way of working these muscles. The legs can be viewed in a similar way in that squatting is excellent for all-round leg strength, but it does not have the refined benefit of using the legs in an event-related way. Therefore lunges, split squats (wide and narrow) and step-up drives

(not heavy step-ups except for very experienced athletes) should be included with or in the place of squats.

Mid-region work should be stressed strongly since this is where most sprinters fail in their strength work. The events require rotational as well as just vertical and linear strength; thus the exercises should reflect this. Any abdominal exercises performed should be matched with an equal amount of work for the back. This should ensure that these muscle groups are strengthened significantly and in a balanced fashion.

Over and above these general exercises, considerable emphasis should be placed on the more specific work. For the arms and shoulders, exercises such as dumb-bell sprint action and alternate standing press are the best, but, if dual pulleys are available, such exercises as alternate pulley punches can be used. For the legs, the several jumping exercises can be performed, as long as the weight is kept low (up to about 50kg maximum). These exercises really do give a considerable increase in all-round leg strength, and also the ability to work very hard for a short period of time, as in the sprints. They have the additional advantage of using the whole legs in a coordinated way that adds to the neuromuscular efficiency relating to the events.

During this strength-phase work it is possible to introduce some simple yet effective plyometric exercises. These can include plyometric half squat jumps, split jumps and calf jumps, as well as low box jumps. Each may be performed with reasonable weight, although the essence of plyometrics is that the speed of response is most important. Thus the weight should be kept at such a level as to maintain a good dynamic response.

The sets and repetitions used should be four sets of from six to ten repetitions, except for the light resistance and body-weight exercises that should have higher repetitions to help with strength endurance. The fixed set/repetition exercises should be geared towards resistance improvement at a constant rate each week. If, however, a particular body segment proves stubbornly weak, it is better to add exercises for that part rather than risk unbalanced development.

## Specific

The specific phase of the schedule is designed around similar exercises to the conditioning and strength phase schedules. The difference is that the sets, repetitions and mental emphasis are all aimed at enhancing competition performance. The starting point is to make sure that the athlete is prepared to start this phase with a dynamic and positive outlook. If this is accomplished, the strength work will be that much easier to benefit from. The actual specific strength-training schedule can include maximum weight lifting on exercises such as clean, snatch and bench press as motivators. The remaining exercises should be aimed at fast work with light weights and low repetitions (four to six sets of four repetitions), including some plyometric work. Timed long sets can also be an interesting addition to this schedule. There is no harm in doing a light strength session one, two or three days before competition, and, in fact, it is now being accepted that specific work the day before a competition can actually enhance the performance. Heavy weights should not be done within at least five days of a race. This is because it takes that long to recover from such work. Some athletes need even longer for their legs to feel loose enough to race, but too much time away from the gym may mean a decline in strength and reactivity. The schedule could therefore consist of two sessions, one a full heavy session, and one with two heavy and five light exercises. How these are used depends on the competition plan, but, during the week leading up to the competition, Monday – light, Wednesday – light is the optimum for most athletes. In non-competition weeks this would revert to Monday – heavy, Wednesday – heavy.

The specific schedule for the sprinter should contain an interesting mixture of elements based on the essential muscle activity inherent in the events. There is great room for flexibility and yet the basics must be covered and maintained, with the added ingredient of psychological urgency intrinsic in dynamic work.

## SUMMARY

The discussion has revolved around the essential structure of the sprinter's schedule. This has been based on the physical needs of the events related to which muscle groups are used. The three phases of training, conditioning, strength and specific are clearly worked out so that the athlete has full knowledge of the type of training he or she is expected to do.

The formulation of each schedule is based on a combination of the phase of training linked to the needs of the events. This leads to the conclusion that certain areas of the body are often under-stressed, a situation which must be resolved if the athlete is to gain the maximum benefits from the training. The aim of strength training for the sprinter is to improve performance generally, enhance the competition results when most required and help in injury prevention. If all of these can be achieved, then the effort will have been worthwhile.

## MIDDLE-DISTANCE EVENTS

The middle-distance events are said to be about 65–75 per cent aerobic and 25–35 per cent anaerobic energy consumption. This masks the need for strength and local muscular endurance, and certain coaches and athletes are still of the opinion that no gains can be made in the gym. This attitude is dying out rapidly since most of the world's great middle-distance athletes adopt some form of strength work. What this should be is at the centre of intense debate, but what is certain is that strength training can help to improve middle-distance performances significantly.

The middle-distance runner works hard at aerobic and general muscular endurance

Fig. 38 Economic middle-distance running. (Dan Grossman)

during the running sessions. However, the gym must be the focus for developing specific and local muscular endurance. The strength training used by the sprinters is applicable to the middle-distance athlete, with the exception of the power work necessary for the sprint start which is unnecessary since the athlete starts in the near erect position.

The emphasis, therefore, must be more on the pulling action of the hamstrings and the gluteus muscles, together with the extension of the ankles by the calves. This, however, does not eliminate the necessity to develop power in the quadriceps as this can add to the final extension of the leg and most particularly during a period of acceleration during a race.

The mid region is one of the most neglected areas in middle-distance athletes and it is here that most injury problems originate. Stiffness and weakness in these muscles produce undue stresses throughout the legs and it is vital that these areas are worked extensively and intensively. Finally, the shoulders and the arms need good, local, muscular endurance as they provide additional drive and balance at crucial stages in the race. It is no coincidence that most of the top middle-distance athletes have significant shoulder development.

How then can we construct relevant schedules to take these elements into consideration? First, it should be stressed that sufficient work can be performed in two sessions per week on strength (although stretching must be performed every day). During conditioning the basic schedule will be similar to that for the sprinter, with the modifications suggested above for the emphasis of exercises. Because only two sessions are to be done per week, a Monday/Thursday or Monday/Friday plan is probably the best. Each session should contain about ten exercises, four sets each, and ten to fifty repetitions in each set. The time between sets can be reduced from

30sec and the rest period between exercises from 45sec to some effect, putting even more emphasis on the aerobic capabilities.

The middle-distance runner needs to be able to accelerate at certain times in the race. This ability comes from being able to switch from aerobic to anaerobic muscle action very rapidly. This can be enhanced by strength training, particularly if the sprint type of work is performed in the gym. The way modern races are run it is essential that this ability is attained and the maximum speed potential is reached by the athlete.

The development of speed depends greatly on the absolute strength of the 320 muscles. This means that, after the initial conditioning phase, the strength phase must be geared in the same way as for the sprinter, although it must be borne in mind that most middle-distance athletes are less bulky than the sprinters and care needs to be taken when setting the resistances. There is, however, nothing wrong with the athlete's being pushed quite hard, and, in fact, this is necessary to make strength gains. It is certainly counterproductive to use only light resistance work since this will merely extend the conditioning phase and become ineffective after a short while.

The specific phase is again similar to the sprinter's in that the exercises are selected on the basis of those used in the events, with emphasis on the legs, middle region and shoulders, and arms. There is no harm in asking the runners to attempt maximum single repetition work, and it is often a welcome change from the running work. The other exercises need to include mid-region near-isometric exercises, jumping exercise and plyometric work to give 'bounce'.

To summarize: the strength training work fits in with the rest of the programme. Two sessions per week are sufficient as long as suppling is performed every day. The three phases of training – conditioning, strength and specific – are operable and the schedules for each are based largely on the sprinter-

Fig. 39 The rigours of cross-country racing. (Dan Grossman)

type work. There is no problem with making the athlete work heavy as long as the technique has been well taught. Even maximum single repetitions may be tried as these represent the ultimate in anaerobic power.

## LONG-DISTANCE AND MARATHON

There is not much to add to the above for the long-distance and marathon athlete except that in most cases the lack of anaerobic ability has lost many races in the very last stages. This indicates that some anaerobic ability is essential, although it is generally accepted that such races are 95 per cent aerobic. There seems little reason why the long-distance runner should not go to the gym for a session or two per week to build up the usually neglected fast fibres. The proviso, as it is with the sprints, middle- and long-distance events, is that strength must increase in relation to body-weight. It would be simply useless to increase body-weight more than strength since the running would get slower.

Thus the long-distance schedules must again be similar to those in sprint-type work, although the emphasis must be similar to that in the middle-distance athlete's schedules. The protection of the back is of utmost importance and mid-region work must therefore be enhanced as far as possible. It is true that, to begin with,

Fig. 40 The steeplechase. (Dan Grossman)

strength training will adversely affect the running training owing to stiffness, but after one or two weeks the benefits will be discovered in newly felt strength and drive.

For the steeplechase additional skill and strength work is needed in order to deal with the barriers. Plyometric strength is needed to perform the hurdling action and additional mid-region strength will certainly assist in this aim. The nature of the event and the necessary additional strengths can be analysed and the relevant activities incorporated in the overall schedule.

## SUMMARY

Strength training can produce remarkable results if performed correctly, even in the marathon. It is most important to ensure that, if a programme is to be adopted, it is integrated into the rest of the training with care. The best results will then be obtained and the body will respond in a positive way. It is also most important that the runner checks on strengths and weaknesses to make sure that they are corrected during strength work. This will ensure that the body develops in a balanced fashion and that persisting weaknesses will be eliminated.

# CHAPTER 6
# Strength Training for Jumping Events

## INTRODUCTION

In Chapter 5 the running events were examined and suggestions were made on how it is possible to analyse the movements in each event to give us the guidelines for the strength-training programme. The jumping events are similar in many ways to the sprints in that they require a maximum strength for weight ratio to provide the greatest height or distance. It is true to say, however, that jumps training needs an additional emphasis on the technical side of a particular discipline. For example, it is clear that the Fosbury high jumper needs significantly different training from the pole vaulter, the action of the former being a non-supported jump with backward rotation and the latter a jump supported by the pole with forward rotation. This sort of consideration is of vital importance when preparing the jumper's schedule.

In addition to the technical side of development we have to consider the fundamental conditioning work that must be done to ensure that the body can take the immense physical and structural pressures of jumping, which seem to take such a heavy toll of athletes. Significantly, not many high jumpers have come out of their careers unscathed by injury, and this is mainly due to incorrect preparation and strength training in the preparatory phase of the jumper's life. This has become more apparent since the introduction of the Fosbury technique which, unfortunately, can be accomplished initially without any additional strength work beyond the body's natural levels. This means that athletes tend to carry on their careers sublimely ignorant of the fact that, as the physical stresses become greater, more strength work needs to be done.

Surprisingly, we find fewer injuries occurring in the triple jump which is, in essence, a far more rigorous test of the body's structure and function than the high jump. This perhaps is a reflection of the fact that, even at a very early stage, the athlete needs special strength to be able to perform the event, in contrast to the high jump. Nevertheless, anyone who has seen front-on film of triple jumpers competing will not have missed the tremendous distortion of the leg which accompanies the landings from the first two phases of the effort. This signifies that, as the distance increases, the specific pressures on the joints increase dramatically. Therefore the coach needs to compensate in the training programme by making sure that the surrounding ligaments and muscles are prepared satisfactorily.

The long jump relates more to the conversion of speed to height than anything else. In this respect the technique is of secondary importance to speed, and only when the athlete can run faster will the distance increase significantly. We have all seen the beautiful technique of the jumper who plops into the pit far short of the crude, fast athlete's mark. This situation has for many years been characteristic of many unsuccessful long jumpers, and it has taken the likes of Carl Lewis to point out the self-evident truth that speed in the long jump means distance. Having said this, it is still essential for the long jumper to do specific work on the take-off to be able to cope with the conversion of energy involved. This is where the performance often goes wrong, with many jumpers having significantly lower angles of take-off than the optimum. This take-off phase is of great significance to all the jumping events and is the point of maximum stress.

The pole vault is no exception, and advances made in take-off technique have led to great increases in the height achieved. This has also seen the type of athlete in the event change from the lighter, smaller individual to the taller and stronger one. This change in itself has necessitated changes in attitude to the programming of the event training. Greater basic and specific strength is now needed to handle the very high handhold positions and faster run-ups. Significantly, as the athletes get bigger so do the poles, and it is not infrequent that 5.30m length poles are seen in international competition. This means that we are really in a new era of vaulting where 6.50m seems

entirely feasible, when only twenty years ago we were agog at 6m. This is perhaps because the athletes are now realizing that one of the main factors determining the height of vault is strength.

## HIGH JUMP

The Fosbury flop is now the universally adopted technique. Its introduction was surely one of the most revolutionary and fundamental changes to have happened in an athletic event. It is similar to the introduction of the O'Brien technique in the shot in the early 1950s and has changed the event fundamentally from its origins. The technique has allowed many more athletes, particularly women, to achieve very reasonable heights. This is because technically it is simple, like the long jump, and can be performed even by very young and inexperienced athletes. Herein lies the problem: because many coaches do not take full cognisance of the fact that, as the height jumped increases, the proportional increase in the pressure on the joints is squared. Thus

Fig. 41 The suppleness of the high jumper. (Dan Grossman)

a 2m high jump is in simple terms around four times more physically demanding than a 1m jump and for each successive increase in height jumped, the body has to be proportionally stronger and stronger at an increasing rate. It may be easy to jump 1m, but 2m is a completely different ball game. This fact cannot be stressed too strongly, because it is at the root of the failure of many talented young jumpers to improve beyond a certain level. For example, how many coaches have strength routines including the rotation in the ankles that is experienced in the take-off for Fosbury? An analysis of the event needs to examine all aspects of the movement to enable a useful and effective strength programme to be developed, thus minimizing possible injury.

The Fosbury has three elements: (i) the run up; (ii) the take-off, and; (iii) the flight over the bar. The run up is closely linked to an increase in the ability to repeat a simple pattern of movement many times to ensure a consistent take-off point. It is largely dependent on the athlete's own physical abilities and will change as the athlete gets stronger and faster. However, as with other technical skills, the correct essential pattern should be taught at an early age and then successively modified, rather than being completely changed. An athlete will naturally run up in a pattern that he or she finds most comfortable, and this is what should be developed rather than a rigid, set path being assumed as the objective for all athletes.

The take-off is the heart of the event and the point of focus for much of the strength training. The movement is one rapid conversion of linear speed into near vertical lift. The athlete achieves this by having the centre of gravity slightly behind the take-off foot, with the knee slightly but significantly bent. At the point of take-off, rotation of the body has already been initiated by the curve of the run up and, by the laws of physics, this rotation continues more rapidly as the foot is planted. Thus, as the athlete jumps,

there is considerable rotational stress on the whole leg, which introduces a rather unnatural response requirement from the muscles. This needs to be worked on, since if all the strength work is linear, little or no strengthening will occur in the rotational movements. This is most significant when you consider the types of strength work advocated in the past for Fosbury jumpers. We saw all the right concepts used in the wrong way. The basic work is, of course, plyometric, but what was used were box jumps, hurdle jumps and so on, which actually bear little resemblance to the actual take-off at all. This is not to say that these activities are entirely useless, more that they form only a small part of the necessary work to improve the take-off. The several rotational jumps and plyometric exercises are far more relevant and should be worked on to ensure minimum injury risk and maximum improvement in take-off power.

In the gym the programme must obviously contain a significant quantity of strength endurance work and should have a high element of dynamic work, rather than the slow, heavy exercises. The general strength part of the programme should be significantly shorter than the specific, but naturally this depends on the coach's analysis of the strength requirements of the individual. The specific phases should contain a high proportion of jumping exercises, all-round body exercises and mid-region work. This would cover the whole event and lead to increases in power while maintaining the body weight at its minimum. Unlike the throwing events, the Fosbury jumper does not need extensive general strength but must bear in mind that all areas of strength have some relevance in the event.

The flight over the bar is of little significance compared with the take-off, as it is purely a technical matter so long as the athlete has worked hard on the mid region. The muscles in this area need to be capable of absorbing the shock of take-off and rotation as well as enabling the athlete to achieve the optimum layout position over the bar. Quite often this cannot be achieved because the stomach muscles are too weak. It must be said, however, that the uncontrolled, hyper-extended, sit-up movement so often advocated by high-jump coaches to strengthen the Fosbury layout position is exceedingly dangerous and can easily damage the back. This type of movement should always be in a totally controlled situation where it is impossible for the athlete to bend too far.

Summing up then, the strength training must be related to the event as far as possible. Such exercises as heavy, wide-stance back squats are of no relevance and may actually be detrimental to the athlete's strength/weight ratio since they build a bulky upper thigh and backside, neither of which is useful. To work the legs it is far better to use feet-touching back squats or, better still, front squats with narrow feet position. In addition, single-leg squats with the rear foot on a bench will significantly improve single leg strength and also enhance confidence under physical stress. Cleans and snatches should also be worked on since these give great increases in all-round dynamic strength. The strength work should be an integral part of the jump training and it is a good idea to do combination sets of weight jumping interspersed by actual jumps. This is a form of mixed set training and developed in usage from the mid 1970s. It is considered to lead to increased coordination transfer between the two activities. It must be said, however, that the strength requirement for the Fosbury technique is far less than that needed to perform the old straddle jump.

Finally then, the pattern of strength training depends on the technique and weaknesses of the individual athlete. It must contain a high proportion of specific work related to the necessary movements in the event. *Heavy, slow work is detrimental to the jumper whereas light, fast-reacting work enhances the plyometric ability of the muscles.* All-round strength and muscular endurance are essential aspects of the strength work. The programme should therefore be worked out on the basis discussed generally for all athletes, with more emphasis being put on the specific and special strength work than on the general.

## LONG JUMP

The long-jump event is in many ways the simplest of the field events, requiring the minimum of technique and the maximum of speed and power. The several movements used to counteract forward rotation in the air are purely secondary to the speed, power and the angle of take-off. This, in essence, means that the long jumper's strength work is geared closely to that of the sprinter, but is enhanced by extra plyometric and power work. Thus, rather than consider plyometrics only in relation to the sprint start, for the long jump we need to work hard at all the strength/response requirements at the take-off.

The concentration on take-off is quite critical since it is at this point that the speed is converted into lift, thus initiating the jump itself. By the time the athlete reaches the board, the optimum speed has been reached with the hips pushed slightly forward. The take-off action is one of applying force to the board for as long as possible. This is accomplished by placing the foot slightly ahead of the body, with a concomitant slight dip of the hips and leg bend. This slight leg bend initiates the stretch response in the quadriceps, which contract rapidly as the centre of gravity passes over the board. The forward movement is maintained by a pulling action developed by the rear-leg muscles and the gluteus group. Thus we have two areas which need specific strength

Fig. 42 The spring of the long jumper. (Howard Payne)

work for the long jump (as well as for the triple jump and the pole-vault). The plyometric activities and the back of the leg work can be integrated into the overall plan with the sprinting strength-development programme.

This is accomplished by constructing a mixed schedule in the strength and specific phases that include all the elements mentioned above. Relating the activity more specifically to the event needs to be done carefully as each athlete will need a different balance of work. For example, one athlete might have strong quads but weak hamstrings, while another might have the opposite. In these two instances, the balance of work in each area would be substantially different. If they were given the same work, the weaknesses would be exaggerated and the improvement would not be as significant.

For all the jumping events the take-off can be mimicked to a certain extent in the gymnasium under controlled conditions. This type of exercise (for example, bench step-up drives for the long and the triple jump) can be developed as necessary, but their inclusion makes a significant contribution to the specific strength increases required.

To summarize: the long-jump strength work is based in the main on a combination of sprint and specific work. This combination must include exercises relating to the muscles used in the take-off. This will maximize the potential for increased distance.

## TRIPLE JUMP

As we discussed earlier, this event is the most rigorous of all athletic events and tends to sort out those athletes actually capable of doing it at a very early stage. This means that the majority of triple jumpers have sufficient strength for the basic movement right from the start. This is most important because it means that strength-training considerations can be geared towards a more general strengthening rather than to remedying weaknesses.

The triple jump is the only event where the full impact of near maximal jumping must be absorbed by the body while still maintaining control and speed for the next phase. This means that significant strength needs to be present for the absorption of force (eccentric) as well as for power production (concentric). The former can be enhanced by controlled box jumping, but it must be stressed that *this activity is not to be engaged in from high boxes before strict and carefully structured conditioning has occurred by using only shallow boxes.* Too often athletes leap off metre-high boxes as the first stage of their plyometric work. This, of course, is ridiculous and more often than not leads to ankle, shin, knee, hip and back injuries. It has been mentioned before that the best way to control plyometric work is in the gym, and this particularly applies in this instance.

Another factor that must be considered when looking at shock absorption and plyometric strength development activities (which must be rigorous for the triple jumper) is that the surface the activities are performed on is most important. Many jumpers get shin soreness and other stress injuries as a result of continuous work on synthetic surfaces. Far less risk is involved by ensuring that many exercises are performed with a soft landing surface, such as matting in the gym, and cinders or grass at the track. It might be said that the jumping surface is hard, but remember that training is just that and needs to be used to enhance performance through many repetitions, which could not be performed safely on a hard or reactive surface.

The strength programme for the triple jumper should contain the elements of sprint work combined with a higher proportion of specific work than is needed for the long

Fig. 43 The power of the triple jumper. (Mark Shearman)

jump. The plyometric exercises need to be combined with shock-absorption work. These activities should be controlled and performed on suitable surfaces to avoid stress injury.

The triple jumper's strength programme must be most carefully constructed, taking full cognisance of the huge physical stresses the event entails. A high level of basic conditioning work is an absolute essential.

## POLE VAULT

This is the most complex of the jumping events because it involves the actual use of the arms as a fundamental part of the basic movement rather than as secondary to it. The pole vaulter needs good arm, shoulder and back strength, as well as the speed and plyometric ability of the long jumper. This is the problem: bulky muscles need to be carried over the bar, but muscles are needed to get the body over. The strength/weight ratio is therefore of vital importance to the vaulter and must be of prime concern when developing the strength programme. There is certainly no room for body fat or extraneous muscle bulk and this must be one of the prime aims in the programme.

The event requires a much more general approach to power development than the others. It is vital that every part of the body is worked on and thus it is most important that the time in the gym is used efficiently. It is too easy to do some work without thinking carefully about time usage, but the amount of strength training needed for the event is so large that, to gain any useful results, the schedules need to be very much

Fig. 44 The nerve of the pole vaulter.

to the point. This means that the exercises used must be related as closely as possible to the event. The inclusion of a high proportion of specific work is therefore vital, and mixed gym and track sessions can be most effective.

The event may be broken down into three main phases: (i) the run up; (ii) the take-off; and (iii) the vault. Each phase needs specific strength to accomplish. The run up is essentially related to sprint work, but it must be taken into consideration that the pole has to be carried. Some work can therefore usefully be done on running with the pole or a weight bar to make the run up as efficient as possible. Nothing can be usefully accomplished at take-off if the athlete is tired out from running up.

The take-off has some of the elements of the long jump combined with tremendous pressure through the back, arms and shoulders. It is clear then that the mid region of the body must absorb the shock and hold firm to conduct the force of take-off. To help this, much useful work can be done on the chinning bar or rope. It is true

to say that pole vaulters need to be competent gymnasts and have similar abilities to them in terms of overall total strength. However, the principles of push/pull with the legs apply as they do with the long jump, and therefore specific legwork to enhance this element needs to be included.

The actual vault requires general strength, but in particular stomach, arm and shoulder strength. This can be achieved through extensive specific work on these areas, again by the use of the chinning bar and ropes. It is clear that, in the end, the pole vaulter needs to work on all areas of strength and power, and therefore has the most difficult job to do of all the jumpers.

In essence, the vaulter needs strength everywhere but in different ways than in any other event. This is why vaulters tend to have great coordination and physical abilities that relate to their event. To enhance these requires careful thought, but, if the correct combination can be worked out, significant improvement can be obtained. It is no use paying lip service to strength training since no useful purpose can be served by wasting time. It is vital that everything is covered as the athlete is only as strong as his weakest part.

## SUMMARY

The jumping events range from the simple long jump to the complex pole vault. They have elements in common as well as individual ones that must be taken into consideration when working out the strength programme. The essential elements include: (i) sprint strength work; (ii) plyometric exercises, and; (iii) general strength work. The proportion of specific work is high because the strength abilities required relate largely to performed movements that are essentially different from normal actions. This does not mean, however, that significant gains cannot be made using fundamental strength training. In common with other explosive events, a three-peak year can be used, and the three phases of the programme also operate (that is, conditioning, strength and specific). Attention must be paid to the fact that more specific work is needed to enhance the plyometric responses of the quadriceps and calf muscles. Probably the most significant requirement for jumpers is to ensure that the body is ready for the stresses that are caused by the nature of the events. This applies particularly to the youngsters, and it is vital that overstress is not introduced by too much bounding and jumping on hard surfaces.

Finally, the jumper must be aware that the wrong strength training will be detrimental to performance and can lead to the apparent perception that strength training does no good. Just remember, think and plan before you train.

## CHAPTER 7
# Strength Training for Throwing Events

## INTRODUCTION

Traditionally, the throwing events have been the focus of strength training, since from the beginning, it was realized that the strongest athlete had the greatest chance of success. In ancient Greece the discus and javelin throwers were the strong men of the Olympic Games. In those days they used to train by wrestling and throwing heavy objects rather than by using any strict strengthening methods. This was left to the modern-era thrower. The greatest advances made in strength training have been made post-war, when it was realized that lifting weights brought about significant strength and distance gains.

At first the schedules were based on simple maximum lifting, but, as interest developed, the bodybuilders tried many different techniques to gain maximal results. In the 1950s most of the basic methods for strength gain were laid down and have not changed significantly since then, except for the modern use of plyometric work in sport. Some of the throwers in that period were vastly strong and their results clearly show this. Such masters as Dallas Long, Randy Matson, Jay Silvester, Ludvig Danek and Janis Lusis all came from this upsurge in the application of strength training to throwing.

The modern thrower gears his or her strength training much more to the specific than previously. This is why we now have a generation of highly athletic and relatively (to the 1960s and 1970s) light throwers.

Looking at the current world's best, we can see how the emphasis has shifted from brute strength to athleticism. This is achieved by making sure that a balance is maintained within the programme and that excessive lifting to the detriment of strength/weight ratio is carefully avoided. As with all other athletic events, speed is the essence of good performance in the throws. The events are grouped with sprints and jumps as explosive. They can therefore be included in those events for which a triple periodized year is effective.

Another key factor is that of flexibility of content in the schedule. Because of the high work load in the thrower's programme, it is essential that the athlete be allowed to work to a level that his or her body feels is right. Too many times athletes fail because they do not listen to their bodies. Many injuries occur because of this and this can be avoided by taking the simple precaution of allowing the athlete to deviate from the set programme if necessary.

The four throwing events – shot putt, discus, hammer and javelin – have increasing implement-release velocities from the first to the last. Thus the general strength factor in the training becomes less significant from the shot through to the javelin. This means that, when analysing the requirements for each, the fact that the release velocity of the implement varies from event to event has to be reflected in the programme.

Similarly, the type of acceleration in each event needs to be looked at. For instance, the fierce acceleration during the shot putt is dissimilar from that during the hammer, which requires a more relaxed, constant increase in speed. This is why most shot putters are bad hammer-throwers and vice versa.

Generally, the thrower needs to work very hard on strength training throughout the year. The development of strength in the correct way will always enhance performance if the technical skills are highly developed too. A common fault in throwing training is the gain of too much general strength before a sound basic technique has been ingrained. This is a fundamental error and can lead to disillusionment at an early age and a frustrating lack of improvement from this imbalance in the training. Young throwers who have made immense strength gains and seen little increase in the distance thrown are often puzzled why this has happened. It often appears that they have worked almost exclusively on lifting, to the near exclusion of technical and athletic improvement. If this is allowed to happen, the results will show just how wrong this approach is.

## SHOT PUTT

The shot putt requires the maximal acceleration of all the athletic events. The implement must be moved from zero speed to release velocity within the 7ft circle. The range actually used is nearer 9 to 10ft (in the linear technique) since the implement is released out from the front of the circle, but nevertheless, the acceleration required is immense and is the key to putting a long way. The power needed to achieve this is made up of the speed of the athlete combined with the strength that can be applied to the shot. Since the weight of the shot is quite high compared with the body mass, each athlete must have a certain amount of sheer mass to avoid being projected backwards during the delivery by reaction to the implement. Thus the object of strength training must be threefold. First, to gain specific strength to apply during the putt. Second, to allow the athlete to get as close to maximum speed during the throw as possible while working against the implement. Third, to increase the mass of the athlete (if required) to minimize the reaction to delivery.

The strength-gain programme must take all this into consideration. Essentially, the putt requires the use of a single-leg hop or turn across the circle, followed by a two-leg drive into the delivery. The delivery phase is a sequential summation of muscular contractions starting with the legs, then the mid region, the shoulders and finally the arms and fingers. This sequential movement is the key to the maximum release velocity and thus the strength programme needs to reflect this.

The start of the year's training should, in common with most other events, be a period of conditioning work. All exercises can be included in this since the throw requires the use of virtually every muscle in the body. The first strength-gain period should be based on a mixture of heavy, slow exercises (for bulking up) and dynamic, technical exercises (to enhance sequential power). These exercises should include bench press (flat and inclined to putting angle), squats (front and back), clean and jerk, snatch, stomach and back work, together with a selection of more specific ones.

The aims should be to increase general strength, put on weight (if required) and maintain or increase speed as far as possible. Plyometrics are not as important for the throws as for the jumps since the muscles must not react too quickly when the throwing position is attained. This might sound contrary to the explosive nature of the event, but, since there is rotation involved in the delivery, if the reaction to landing is

Fig. 45 The explosion of the shot putter.

immediate this cannot be effected properly. More significant is the use of non-plyometric versions of the jumping exercises, such as squat jumps or split jumps, but these are best left to the specific training that follows the strength phase. In addition to these considerations is the fact that, during the glide or turn, the athlete tries to maintain the position of the body isometrically to maximize wind-up. Therefore some work should be included in the schedules to allow this to be performed with the minimum of effort. Such exercises as glides or turns with a barbell on the shoulders are an effective way to accomplish this.

The first specific phase should be geared towards three activities: (i) maintenance of strength; (ii) increasing speed and; (iii) improving specific capabilities in relation to technique. The first is achieved by working on pyramid lifting to twos and singles. This is a key part of the work since it gives the athlete an enhanced ability to respond to the one-off effort required in competition. Speed is increased by losing the few extra pounds gained in the first strength phase and by working on light, fast weights. The specific capabilities will be enhanced by performing exercises that relate to the technical requirements of the athlete. Such exercises as shot press, glides with a 20lb bar on the shoulders, single-arm dumbbell jerk and similar, will make the strength work relate more directly to the movements of the event. The purpose of the specific strength work, as with the other events, is to tune the athlete to maximal performance during competition, and it should be remembered that, if the athlete is tired, he or she will not perform well. Therefore some leeway for change must be included in this phase, depending on the needs of each athlete.

The second strength phase is slightly different from the first, in that during it two sub-phases are included. The first is based on general strength gain by using squat, bench press and dead lift type exercises (heavy, slow), followed then by a second sub-phase where the emphasis is on the power exercises, clean and jerk, snatch and squat jumps. This then links in with the second specific phase that is the same as the first.

To achieve the third peak there must be an intermediate phase between specific two and three. This should be a period of training that alleviates the pressure of competition and refreshes the athlete ready for the final high point of the year. It may include anything that the coach thinks will serve as a change in routine, such as the inclusion of different exercises or a different sets and repetitions plan. The final specific phase is the same as the others, gearing the strength work to maximize performance.

Essentially then, the strength training requirements for the shot are probably the most intense of any event. The athlete needs massive general and specific strength while maintaining great athleticism. The delicate balance between strength, body weight and speed needs to be optimal for maximum performance. It is therefore vital that the coach constantly reviews the programme to make sure that nothing is going wrong.

## DISCUS THROW

The discus event is similar in many ways to the rotational shot putt except that the athlete has longer to accelerate the implement. Greater relaxation is also needed to ensure the maximum effective range for applying force. This relaxation is mostly needed to keep the discus well behind the hips during the turn into the throwing position. As a consequence of this long range implicit in a good throw, the thrower needs to be very strong over the same range. Thus it is vital that, particularly in the shoulders, total mobility in the joints is

Fig. 46 The discus release.

maintained and strength exercises are performed over the full range.

The discus throw has some specific requirements over and above the range of movement factor. These are related to the rotational nature of the technique commonly used. The rotation means that the mid region comes in for a lot of hammering during the throw, and many discus throwers succumb to back injuries through not being sufficiently conditioned there. Such exercises as disc rotations, barbell rotations and hanging leg rotations are all an essential part of the discus thrower's armoury of strength exercises. They must be performed throughout the year to help avoid mid-region injuries.

The complete programme follows a similar pattern to that for the shot. The general strength work is not as extensive, except in the strength one phase. The discus requires considerable pulling ability, which is enhanced by extra work on snatch, clean and pulls, exercises which assist the delivery. Unlike the shot, the discus delivery is essentially a pulling movement and, apart from working on the basic exercises, arm pulling work with dumbbells and pulleys strengthens the arms and shoulders specifically. This means that, during the specific as well as the strength phase, such exercises can be used to keep the technical side of the event closely related to the strength work.

Working the other way round, heavy discus and weight disc throwing have also been used to build specific strength. Care must be taken to ensure that this does not affect the actual technique, and certainly turns should not be done with an implement weighing more than 25 per cent over the normal weight. Standing throws may, however, be effectively performed with much heavier resistance.

The discus is similar to the hammer in its rotational footwork and likewise needs smooth, relaxed acceleration in the circle. The muscle tone and strength in the legs needed to accomplish this are enhanced by significant periods of jumping with medium and light resistances. This work may effectively be done at any time during the year, but it is an essential element of the specific phases. As with all the throws, the discus thrower must be athletic as well as strong. Jumping improves this quality significantly.

The discus strength programme then is essentially the same as the shot putter's except that more emphasis is put on the dynamic pulling activities as specific work. The bulking-up phase is less likely to be significant since the implement does not create as much reaction in the body as does the shot. Dumbbells and pulleys may be used to great effect in the specific phases of training. During these it is vital that flexibility of approach is included in the programme since the athlete must be able to vary the work depending on the state of his or her body. Few throwers will have to be told to work harder but some may need to be slowed down.

## HAMMER THROW

The hammer is the odd event out in this particular group. This is because it is the only throw in which the hips do not lead the

Fig. 47 The back strength of the hammer thrower. (Howard Payne)

shoulders to any significant extent. This means that the acceleration of the implement is effected by short but very rapid, two-footed, support-phase, downward pulls during the turns. This employs the strong muscles of the back operating almost isometrically, rather than an active hip drive. To deal with this, the hammer thrower needs far more back strength than in the other throws. This can be gained by an emphasis on heavy pulling movements, such as clean, snatch, dead lift and pulls. This is supplemented with much front and back squatting, but the rotational acceleration pattern must not be ignored.

The full programme has the same pattern as in the shot, except that the emphasis is much more on the pulls than the pushes. The hammer does not contain any element of push, but for balance in musculature some of the work must be included. Probably the best exercise to use is the standing press or jerk, which will aid the fierce drive during the delivery.

The hammer is a difficult event for which to work out the strength training because of the rotational emphasis during the turns. There is a high isometric element that should be taken into consideration when constructing the schedules. This can best be worked on by performing such exercises as hammer turns with a barbell on the shoulders or a weight at arm's length. The isometric tension can be held for longer than the normal optimum of 6sec, because the effort is not maximal. Holding the positions for about 12 to 15sec produces good results.

Another area that needs special attention is the mid region. There are many good exercises which may be used for this, such as lying and standing disc rotations, inclined disc rotations and rotating leg raises. All such work has a beneficial effect on the strength level in the mid region which is so essential for good throwing. It must be remembered, however, that range of movement must not be sacrificed in order to gain strength. The body must be supple as well as strong.

For the delivery, the best exercise is probably the narrow-grip snatch and the rotating dumbbell snatch. These mimic the delivery quite closely and the rotation can be introduced to get it even closer. Most hammer throwers are good at the Olympic lifts and this is an indication of the necessary emphasis of the strength-training schedule. However, the actual turns must not be ignored, and these perhaps contribute the most towards the ultimate distance achieved.

To summarize: the hammer can be considered as a pulling event. It must therefore be treated as such for strength-training purposes and the exercises chosen accordingly. The Olympic lifts must be an essential part of the schedules, as should some isometric exercises to help the maintenance of the position during the turns. Apart from this, the essential programme resembles that for shot in that strength work must be the most important element. Much effective specific work can be achieved by throwing heavy weights and hammers.

## JAVELIN THROW

The javelin throw requires the greatest release velocity of the throws and this must be taken into consideration when the strength requirements are worked out. Most modern javelin throwers have introduced considerable rotation into the throw and this is an additional factor to be looked at. Unlike the other throws, the pre-delivery movement is not restricted to a small circle. This means that the throw is made up of three elements: (i) the run-up; (ii) the transition phase and; (iii) the delivery.

The run up is closely similar to that in the pole vault in that the implement has to be carried during the run. Because the javelin is only light, there is little modification in

Fig. 48 The flexibility of the javelin thrower. (Howard Payne)

balance and the technique of running but, nevertheless, it must be practised. To minimize the inconvenience of carrying the javelin, a heavier object may be used to acquaint the body with the sensation. In addition, this helps to build the isometric strength in the necessary muscles which leads to greater control during the transition phase.

When the athlete wishes to prepare for delivery, he must pass through a sequence of movements that convert the frontal run up into an effective delivery position. This is the transition phase. The element of greatest importance here is that of control; this can be enhanced by the work mentioned above.

To attain an effective delivery position, the thrower must have significant leg and mid-region strength. These are the main areas where strength training can be of benefit for this phase. Jumping with or without weights is of particular relevance and should be an integral part of both the strength and the specific phases. The delivery itself is a complex combination of movements, ending with a rapid pull of the javelin with the arm. The sequence of acceleration is similar to that in the shot in that there is a summation of muscular power starting with the legs and ending with the arm and the hand. Because of this, the strength work must be geared mainly to sequential exercises such as the Olympic lifts. Less emphasis needs to be placed on the heavy, slow, general exercises and, although squatting will help, jumping with weights is far better in both the strength and the specific phases.

The general concept of strength development should thus be one of producing sequential, rapid power. The body/weight factor has little relevance in the javelin and so the thrower may be light and still suffer no penalty in the delivery. This means that in the programme, unlike as in the shot, considerable time can be spent on fast, lighter movements.

Because of the tremendous power development in the delivery, the thrower must pay particular attention to the mid region and core stability. Recently, a heavier emphasis has been applied to these with the use of specific exercises in which the body is held isometrically while the arms are worked throwing heavy objects. These combination exercises emphasize the importance of maintaining body position while performing movements around the fixed body segments. This is actually common to all throws before the final delivery and such exercises may effectively be included in the programmes for all the events.

To conclude then, the javelin event is the odd one out of the throws in that it has an unlimited run up. This means that running strength is an important factor in the programme. In addition, emphasis must be placed on rapid and coordinated exercises to maximize the release speed. The required programme is similar to that for the shot but it must be influenced by similar considerations as for the long jump or the pole vault.

## SUMMARY

The throwing events are historically the most advanced in the athletic programme in relation to strength training. They utilize all the facets of strength training at some time or another, and thus the coach needs to be fully conversant with the whole area of strength training and its applications. Each event is unique but, generally, it is vital that strength training is a significant part of the training programme. It is necessary to bear in mind, however, that strength must be relevant to the event and not merely general. To this end the use of recently developed specific and special strength techniques is of particular significance. It must be remembered that the thrower should be the Greek god of athletics rather than the sumo wrestler. Speed, athleticism and strength must be combined to produce a true, world-class thrower.

# CHAPTER 8
# Power Development

## WHAT IS POWER?

Fig. 49 Split clean.

From earlier chapters we have seen that power is the product of speed multiplied by strength. It is the essential ingredient for all athletes since the development of speed to its near maximum can be achieved only if the muscles have sufficient strength. As the strength increases, the power increases too, assuming that the range of movement does not decrease. The power of an athlete is in many ways quite specific. For example, a thrower may develop considerable power by virtue of increasing his weight with his strength. This amount of power would be useless to a middle-distance runner who must minimize body weight so that the anaerobic and aerobic systems are at their most efficient.

Therefore power must relate to body weight. The concept of power to body-weight ratio gives us the ability to compare states of power during an athlete's career. But how is this measured? This is a most difficult question to answer since absolute speed and strength are meaningless concepts when talking about movements in specific events. We can obtain a near approximation by using the standing long- and triple-jump tests. Since these involve moving the athlete's body weight, they are simple tests for assessing the power/body weight ratio. These are also excellent indicators of basic power in relation to body weight and can be used as an assessment tool for the results of training.

## HOW POWER IS DEVELOPED

The two constituents of power, speed and strength, can be improved but to very different extents. Speed is inherited and no amount of training will improve the given level more than about 10 per cent. It must be understood that the intrinsic muscle speed and the speed of running are different quantities. Thus running speed can improve significantly more than 10 per cent because it is affected, not only by the inherent speed, but also by range and strength of movement. The intrinsic speed, however, is a quantity set in stone at birth and relates only to physiological parameters such as the type of muscle fibre which predominates. This is why only a small improvement can be attained; this is due to slight improvements in efficiency within the physiological systems.

Strength, on the other hand, can be increased by up to around 400 per cent over its original level. This is effected by utilizing the adaptation process which comes into effect when resistance is applied to moving. This process causes the muscle fibres to break down. When the fibres regenerate they are larger than before. This makes the whole muscle bigger than previously. Concurrent with these changes, the fat in the connecting tissue is removed and the muscle becomes smaller and more clearly defined. Thus, initially at least, there is little change in total muscle size but a marked increase in definition. This is to the advantage of the athlete since it means that there is less 'useless' weight to carry around and the power/body-weight ratio increases.

The problem that arises with most sportsmen and women is that the strength levels increase but not enough specific coordination work is done to link that strength with speed. This means that the strength is actually a hindrance rather than an advantage. Thus specific power exercises are needed to ensure the maximal increase in power. The important factor relates more to the way the exercises are performed rather than to technical differences. It has always been considered that fast exercises are better than slow ones at increasing power. This has been an assumption rather than a proven fact until recently, since when it has been clearly shown that the fast muscle fibres, which are responsible for fast actions, develop more with rapid training activities. This relates to the neuromuscular system and the anaerobic metabolic pathways.

The neuromuscular pathways arise in the cerebrum and pass through the cerebellum, which refines the messages to the muscles. From there they pass down the spinal cord and out through the peripheral nerves to the muscles. The nerves are made up of bundles of nerve cell fibres. These bundles split up as they enter the muscle and each fibre goes to a muscle fibre or group of fibres. The messages are transmitted across the nerve–muscle gap by chemical transmitters that change the nature of the muscle fibre membrane, which, in turn, allows the flow of inorganic ions in the reverse balance to the uncontracted state. This causes the muscle to shorten by changing the protein structure, as was discussed earlier. This whole system makes up the neuromuscular pathway needed to use a muscle. The only way it can be improved is through constant use, which seems to improve the general efficiency of the system, probably by improving the biochemical activity and the ability of the membranes to transfer the ions. Suffice it to say that this improvement is only by about 10 per cent and no way has been found to increase this with training.

The anaerobic metabolism which relates to strength is a different matter. Great improvements can be effected by training. These are based on the response of the cells to anaerobic activity. The body is highly adaptable and, if you apply stress to it, there is an adaptive response, at first by changing the instantaneous metabolism and then, if the stress persists, long-term changes occur. These are based on increases in certain enzymes that control the production of the several energy sources.

The big question is, how do we initiate these changes in the practical situation? This has been studied extensively and it is now accepted that, over and above the standard strength-training work outlined in previous chapters, there are effective ways of increasing power. One of Poland's best throws coaches put forward a concept of power training in the mid-1980s. He put a clear emphasis on a hard power session. This involved the use of light resistance work performed at maximum speed with minimum rest. The details of his sessions were not fully elucidated. As a result, I conducted some experiments on the general concept but with the specific content related to what my athletes were already performing.

## THE WINCH POWER SESSIONS

The most effective sessions, as measured by improvement in standing jump distances, comprised seven exercises, each performed at maximum speed but within the limit of 6sec for five repetitions. The resistance was to match these parameters as closely as possible. Six sets of each exercise were performed at maximum speed, with 10sec rest between each. Before the next exercise was started, 30sec rest was allowed. Needless to say, at the first attempt most athletes reached complete exhaustion since the pulse rate rose to 180+ and stayed there for the full session apart from small falls in between exercises.

This scheme has now been used over the years and has proved to be an effective power development tool, being refined along the way for specific events and event groups. The exact content of the session is varied depending on the event, but in the main the exercises are fairly similar. Here are examples of the session I have used for sprints and shot putt:

*Session 1: Sprints*
1. hang clean and press
2. alternate dumbell press
3. upright rowing (or narrow split jumps for extra leg work)
4. chinnies (left plus right = one repetition)
5. squat jumps
6. inclined sit ups
7. hang snatch

*Session 2: Shot putt*
1. hang clean and press
2. chinnies
3. bent-over rowing
4. bench press
5. narrow split jumps
6. flying exercise
7. hang snatch

Each set is timed so that a complete record of the sessions can be used for future comparison. The recovery times are applied strictly to ensure consistency from session to session. At the end, the pulse is taken for 5min to give information on the recovery rate, since sometimes problems can be highlighted before they go too far. These usually show up in the pulse recovery that tends to be very slow when the athlete has problems, such as infections or over-training. The resistance is increased for the following session if the times per set for an exercise are too short (below 5sec).

What I have found when this session is performed once per week is that there is a significant increase in power as measured by using the standing jumps. This applies to throwers, sprinters and jumpers, and appears to be independent of what other training is being performed at the time. This would suggest that the session stimulates part of the muscle system that is not affected to any great extent by any other type of training. This power session must therefore be considered to be a significant adjunct to peaking, since a predictable improvement can be obtained. Because of this, I would suggest that it is used in the lead up to a peak in conjunction with the specific training.

The process behind the action of the power session seems to relate to the fact that the athlete is working anaerobically at maximum stretch for the duration. This is a powerful stimulus for the body's enzymic systems as well as the neuromuscular axis. The immediacy of the effect suggests that the change in systems is quite dramatic. Interestingly, the sessions last only just over 10min, a great return for so short a time. This is a clear indication that the intensity of training is more relevant than the total amount performed. This is borne out by a trend in middle-distance running using a lower mileage but a higher intensity.

## OTHER POWER WORK

Over and above the session above, combined power and strength work can be effectively performed in the standard strength programme. This relates to the way the exercises are performed as well as which ones are used. Most athletes include cleans and snatches in their work. These are most effective exercises and can aid power development significantly. This is exemplified by the fact that many throwers are also high-ranking weightlifters and that many world-class runners can clean well over their body weight.

It would seem therefore that the fast dynamic movements with weights can enhance power in most athletes. These exercises do not add significantly to their bulk, as do the slower squat and bench-press exercises, but even these may be of use in power training if performed dynamically.

Fig. 50 Speed shown in the power snatch, seen from the front.

## SUMMARY

The essence of athletic performances in the explosive events, and to some extent in the others as well, is the development of power. By power we mean the combination of speed and strength. The first of these cannot be increased more than about 10 per cent, whereas strength can be improved by around 400 per cent.

Therefore the most effective way to improve power is to increase strength by performing fast exercises such as cleans and snatches. Specific power sessions can be devised to give a very significant boost to measurable power. The simplest way to measure such changes as power/body-weight ratios and also those derived from general training is to use the standing jumps.

In view of the importance of power, as opposed to absolute strength, consideration must be given to the most effective way of developing it. This must include all the factors mentioned above, with the addition of the high-level power sessions running up to the required peaks. Remember that it is better to change your schedule rather than persevere with sessions that do not improve your power/weight ratio. Only in the throws is absolute strength of equal importance to this ratio, and then probably only in the shot does the body weight need to be quite high to absorb the reaction of the implement on release.

The modern athlete needs to be a Greek god not an ox. This is clearly seen in the modern-day athletes whose superb physiques and power cannot be questioned.

# CHAPTER 9
# Basic Exercises

## INTRODUCTION

There are many exercises that are used in the strength training of athletes. These may be broadly categorized as: all-round, leg extending, leg flexing, abdominals, back, chest and arm pushing, and arm pulling.

These regions constitute the major strength areas of the body and there are a myriad of exercises to develop each. Over and above the actual exercises there are, of course, different ways of performing them, as has been explained in previous chapters. Here we shall confine ourselves to the actual exercises and the key points in their performance.

It is vital that each exercise is performed technically in the correct manner, since not only does this ensure safer exercising but also the maximum improvement in results. Some time must be spent on each exercise in learning how to do it properly, and *heavy resistance should not be attempted until good technique has been achieved.*

The breathing pattern during each exercise is most important. For general strengthening, immediately before starting each repetition a deep breath is taken. The air is exhaled only after the effort has been made. This is because the intake of air stabilizes the thorax and helps to prevent damage to the spine.

## ALL-ROUND STRENGTHENING EXERCISES

### Power Cleans

The basic form of this exercise is the power clean, which is the most fundamental of all the lifts with weights and has a special place in the repertoire in view of its use as part of the so-called Olympic lifts. Historically, it derived from the old-time circus strongmen who used to demonstrate how much weight they could lift by using a similar technique.

The feet are placed under the bar so that it is over the insteps. The hands grip the bar at about shoulder width apart. The initial position is then adopted by sitting down towards the bar with a straight back (not vertical). The eyes are fixed parallel with the ground and the arms are kept locked straight. In its simplest form the bar is lifted in one movement to the shoulders, passing as close to the body as possible. As the bar brushes the thighs, a concerted effort is made to accelerate it. This is called the second pull, the first pull being from the ground to the thighs. The bar is caught at the shoulders by a quick wrist rotation that puts the arms in a supporting position by the shoulders. Simultaneous with this is a slight knee bend to make sure that the joints are not jarred when the bar is caught. The bar is safely lowered by reversing the whole

Figs 51–53 Power clean.

## Power Snatch

The power snatch is the basic form of this lift and, in essence, is similar to the power clean except that the bar is lifted from the ground to the arms extended overhead position. The first position is the same as for the clean except that the grip is much wider (15–25cm wider with each hand). This means that the back is rather more bent forward but it is still kept straight. Because of this initial position, the first part of the movement is a little slower than for the clean, and thus the second pull from the thighs is more marked. The bar must be received with the arms locked, and a frequent mistake is to try to push the bar into its final position. This should not be attempted since it puts undue stress on the back. Because the bar is so high at the end of the movement, there are often balance problems. It is therefore vital that the movement is practised with a light weight to make sure that the technique and the

process and should never be dropped by relaxing the back into an arch, because this may cause injury. The back is kept straight throughout the movement.

Advanced forms of this exercise can be developed. These are: the squat clean, in which the lifter moves to the full squat (knees bent) position to receive the bar, and the split clean, in which the feet are moved into the split (forward and back) position to receive the bar. These should be attempted only by the experienced lifter.

Figs 54–57 Power snatch.

## Dead Lift

balance are learned before any heavy weights are attempted. In common with the clean, both squat and split advanced versions of this exercise can be attempted. These are technically difficult movements and require considerable learning and practice time to achieve competence.

This exercise is probably the strongest of all fundamental movements with weights. It simply involves the lifting of the bar from the ground to the waist. The movement is started in the clean position but then the bar is simply kept at arm's length and hauled up to the legs and back vertical position. Since a lot of weight can be handled, beginners should not attempt it until they have done several months of cleaning, which strengthens all the muscles involved without straining them too much. Dead lift is the cause of many back injuries through strength trainers trying to overload the body without the necessary preparatory conditioning.

## Hack Lift

This is performed in a similar manner to the dead lift except that the bar is placed behind the legs at the starting point. It should rest comfortably against the back of the calves. Some athletes have problems with this position, in which case some flexibility work may be needed to ensure a safe and effective lift. From this starting position the athlete stands, pulling the bar up the back of the legs to a fully erect position. Care must be taken to ensure that the weight is not so

heavy that the bar is dragged up the back of legs with heavy contact. Position is most important in this lift. When done correctly it can be a great strengthener of the back and legs.

## LEG-EXTENDING EXERCISES

### Back Squat

The back squat is the most basic of the leg-extending exercises. It strengthens the whole of the legs as well as the back. It involves taking the bar on the back of the shoulders and squatting down with a straight back (not vertical) and the eyes looking slightly above parallel with the ground. The depth of the squat depends on the requirements, but the limit for athletes should be to the point

Figs 58&59 Hack lift.

Figs 60–62 Back squat from the front.

Figs 63–65 Back squat from the side.

where the tops of the thighs are parallel with the ground. Most athletic events need leg strength to this level and it is a mistake to assume that, since the activity requires only a 45-degree leg flexion, that strengthening should be acquired only over the same range. Certainly, strength is needed beyond this range to give the athlete the ability to work comfortably within and even beyond the required range.

Figs 66–68 Front squat.

The back squat is the best leg-strengthening exercise for general purposes and is also the safest. It must be remembered, however, that the exercise must be done correctly since if it is not, the back, knees and hips may be injured. It is vital that, for beginners, a lengthy period of light resistance work is done to make sure that the correct pattern of movement is acquired before any heavy resistance work is attempted.

### Front Squat

This type of squat works the quadriceps and the upper back more than does the back squat. It is of considerable use to the athlete because the areas that it develops are those more closely associated with dynamic movement of the body. It is, however, much more difficult to perform because the bar is

supported on the shoulders at the front in a similar position to that used to receive the bar in the power clean. The hands support the bar and, as a result, quite a lot of stress is put on the wrists. This is a problem for the beginner who often finds the exercise too painful to perform. To alleviate this problem, the hand may be rested crossed over above the bar. To do this and still hold the bar firmly in position, the elbows need to be held strictly in front and not allowed to drop. As with other movements, it is important that only a light resistance is used to begin with until the athlete feels comfortable with the movement.

## Leg Extension

This exercise is a most useful addition to the strength-training programme because it is the most effective way of isolating the

ii

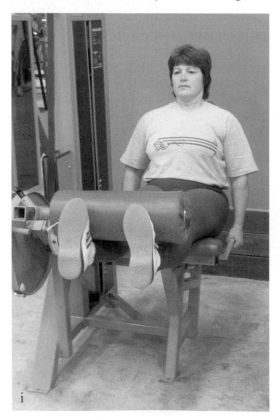

i

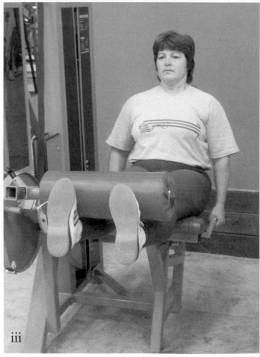

iii

Figs 69–71 Leg extension.

quadriceps muscles. In itself, it is not much use for developing the coordinated leg strength needed for athletic movements, but it is efficacious in producing extra leg strength in this most vital area. To perform the exercise most efficiently the athlete must sit up at the machine, as shown in the photographs. The legs are then extended and the top position held for 2sec. This is because, if the movement is performed without the pause, the resulting swinging movement has little strengthening effect.

## LEG-FLEXING EXERCISES

### Leg Biceps Curl

This exercise is performed on the same machine as the leg extension. It works the hamstrings, gluteus and lower back muscles and is a good antagonist exercise to leg extensions. It may be used for the rehabilitation of these muscles and also to develop considerable strength. The athlete lies on the bench with the body face-down and flat. This is to ensure that the backside does not lift during the exercise. The bar is pulled towards the head and held at the top position for a second, again to avoid the swinging action. It is then returned to the starting position, making sure that the hamstrings are fully relaxed before another attempt is made.

A similar exercise may be performed without a machine, by a second person applying the resistance. It is important to remember, however, that, if this is attempted, steady and controlled pressure must be applied. Any jerking or violent pulling will cause injury.

Squats actually work the same muscles quite strongly, so these exercises are not essential if time is limited. They should be used if specific strengthening is required.

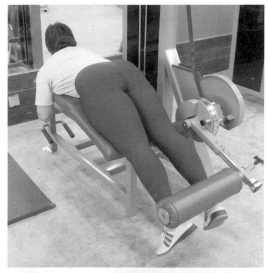

Figs 72–74 Leg bicep curl.

Figs 75–79 Inclined twisting sit-ups.

## ABDOMINAL EXERCISES

### Inclined Twisting Sit Ups

Sit ups are probably the most universally performed exercise. They work and strengthen the abdominal muscles and there are many variations on the elementary movement. Essentially, the most effective way to perform them is on an inclined bench to provide a constant but variable resistance. The knees should be kept bent during the exercise to reduce strain on the lower back and reduce the use of the hip flexors.

In addition to the straight up and down movement, a twist to left and/or right can be introduced to work the oblique and transversus muscles. This type of rotation is useful for athletes since all events contain some such movement. It is most important not just to work the central abdominals but to improve the strength of the surrounding muscles. If a resistance is used during sit ups, it is vital to ensure that the back is kept curved rather than straight. As with bent knees, this reduces back stress. There are many more variations on the basic sit-up movement and a selection of them can be performed within the total schedule.

ii

## Inclined Leg Raises

Leg raises are the opposite movement to sit ups in that the body is fixed and the legs are raised and lowered. This is best done on an

iii

i

Figs 80–82 Inclined leg raises.

inclined bench, but it can be performed on the flat, hanging from chinning bars or on a bench to get additional range, although care must be taken not to hyperextend the back excessively. The straight-leg version of this exercise puts considerable stress on the lower back, so it is important that no one with back problems attempts it. If leg raises are performed with the knees bent, this reduces the danger and can be a useful way of working the abdominal muscles and hip flexors for all athletes. Slight rotation may be introduced and even a circling action, which works the oblique and transversus muscles in addition to the central abdominals. It is probably better to increase the resistance by increasing the angle at which the exercise is performed rather than by applying weight to the feet.

## Seated Disc Rotations

This is an excellent exercise for increasing the range of rotational movement and strength in the back. The athlete sits on a bench with legs astride and tight in to prevent any hip and leg movement during the exercise. A light disc (5–10kg) is held in front with the elbows tucked tight into the sides and the body held erect. From here the athlete rotates to one side, stops and then tries to move further. The final point is held for 2sec and then the body is rotated to the

ii

iii

i

other side, held in a pause and turned further. This position is again held for 2sec. This is repeated the required number of times. No movement of the hips and legs is allowed and the final positions left and right are held as tightly as possible for maximum effect.

Figs 88–90 Back hyperextensions.

Figs 83–87 Seated disc rotations.

## BACK EXERCISES

### Back Hyperextensions

This exercise strengthens the lower and mid back muscles as well as the gluteus and hamstrings. It is performed by lying flat on the floor with the hands behind the head.

The back is then arched, lifting the shoulders and legs off the ground. The top position is held for 2sec before the starting position is resumed. The shoulders are raised only slightly above the horizontal since any further range might aggravate the vertebral joints. Slight rotation can be introduced but this makes the exercise more difficult to perform.

Back hyperextensions can also be performed lying over a bench with the feet fixed. The body is lowered so that the head just touches the ground. From here the body is arched back under complete control since any swinging may cause too much hyperextension to occur with danger to the lower back. The body should be raised to a position only just above the horizontal to maximize safety. The top position is held for 2sec and the body is then lowered back to the ground. It is vital that, in all back hyperextension exercises, a final position is achieved which puts no excessive stress on the lower back.

## Bent-Over Rowing

Figs 91–93 Wide grip bent-over rowing. (left)

Figs 94–96 Narrow grip bent-over rowing. (above)

This exercise strengthens the middle and the upper back and is a good general back exercise that can be performed by any athlete safely. The bar is initially dead-lifted to the waist. From here the legs are slightly bent and, keeping the eyes parallel with the ground, the body is bent to the horizontal position with the bar at arm's length and the back held straight. Attaining this position can be difficult and practice with no resistance is sometimes needed to ensure good technique. There should be no movement of the back during the exercise so that the back muscles are used solely in moving the bar. The bar can be gripped wide or narrow and can be pulled to the chest or stomach depending on what emphasis is required. The exercise is effective in counterbalancing those that develop the chest.

## Upright Rowing

This exercise mainly develops the medial deltoid, upper back and trapezius muscles and is performed in a fixed standing position. The bar is held at the waist with a

Figs 97–99 Upright rowing.

narrow grip, and then pulled to the chin and held there for a second. No rocking motion

Figs 100–102 Bench press.

at the waist is allowed since this reduces the effectiveness of the movement. The end position should be as high as possible with the elbows held above the head. As the bar is lowered again to the waist an effort is made to relax the shoulders and thus maximize the range of pull.

## CHEST AND ARM-PUSHING EXERCISES

There are many exercises that work the muscles of the chest and arms. This is because aesthetically the body looks better if these are developed and, as a result, most non-sporting strength trainers and body-builders concentrate on these areas. The most often used are the arm-pushing exercises.

### Bench Press

This is the simplest of all exercises. It is performed by lying on a bench with the feet firmly placed on the floor. The bar is taken at arm's length, lowered to the chest and then pushed back up to arm's length. If a narrow grip is used the triceps and deltoids are predominantly worked, a medium grip exercises the triceps, deltoids and pectorals, and a wide grip develops the pectorals mainly. The exercise can be performed with a pause at the chest or a slight bounce. If

i

ii

dumbbells are used rather than a barbell, extra range is obtained which strengthens all the muscles more effectively. If the bench is inclined the emphasis moves to the upper pectorals and deltoids. This is useful for the throwers who tend to project the implement closer to 35 degrees to the horizontal rather than straight in line away from the body.

Because the bench press works the whole chest, shoulder and arm-pushing muscles, the exercise is of great use to most athletes in general strengthening.

### Press Behind Neck

This exercise increases shoulder and arm strength in the overhead movement. It is safer than the front press, which tends to put much pressure on the lower back. It is performed by holding the bar on the shoulders behind the head, as for the back squat. From here, the bar is pushed to arm's length and then lowered back to the shoulders. It is important to make sure that

iii

Figs 103–105 Press behind neck.

the body is rigid and stable. Any backward or forward swaying leads to undue pressures on the back. The exercise may also be performed sitting down, which reduces the possibility of incorrect movement.

## ARM-PULLING EXERCISES

### Biceps Curls

This is the bodybuilder's favourite exercise. It is performed by holding a bar at waist height with the hands facing the front,

Figs 106–108 Arm biceps curl.

shoulder width apart. From here the bar is 'curled' to the neck with the minimum of rocking and then lowered back to the waist. The exercise has many variations, such as using dumbbells or reversing the grip. Most of these still work the biceps predominantly, but they add interest to any session.

### Flying Exercise

This is a most useful exercise for athletes since it strengthens the chest, shoulders and biceps at the same time. It is performed with dumbbells which are held at arm's length while the athlete lies on a bench as in the bench press. From here the weights are lowered with slightly bent arms to the floor. From there they are raised in an arc to the starting position. It is important, particularly when heavy weights are being used, to keep the elbows slightly flexed. This reduces elbow strain and gives a stronger movement.

A light, straight-arm version may be used to great effect, particularly by discus throwers, but only by experienced athletes. When performed on an inclined bench, the exercise is of most benefit because the angle

of movement is close to the implement-release angle.

Figs 109–112 Flying exercise.

## SUMMARY

The exercises discussed above are general in nature and have been selected to give the beginner some indication of the movements that are required to start on the road to strengthening the body. There are many variations on each exercise which, if used, can make the sessions more specific as well as less boring. Remember that it is vital to perform the exercises correctly to gain the greatest advantage and reduce the risk of injury.

# CHAPTER 10
# Specific Event Exercises

## INTRODUCTION

Following on from the general strength exercises described in the last chapter, we now look at some specific exercises for the individual events and event groups. This use of specific exercises gives us the opportunity not only to vary the schedule contents but also to make relevant, specific contributions to the strength levels in particular event stress areas. It is not enough just to have general strength; it is vital that the exercises used as specific strengthening are simple, safe and relevant.

The exercises discussed below are only a small selection of those that are available, but they should give you a clear indication of the types of movement that can be used and developed. As has been said earlier, each athlete is unique and it is therefore important for both athlete and coach to learn and to overcome specific weaknesses. Specific strengthening work is the best way to do this and can be included at any stage of the programme as well as during the predefined, specific phases.

The exercises described are in event groups or single events, depending on the technical specificity.

## RUNNING, HURDLING AND WALKING EVENTS

The running events require specific work to be performed on the legs particularly, but often there are severe weaknesses in the stomach and the back. These are what cause so many runners to end up with back problems. Considerable emphasis must therefore be placed on the mid region if the athlete is to remain free from the trauma of back pain and its consequent complications. Since running contains a considerable element of hip rotation it is obvious that purely symmetrical mid-region work is not going to be specific to the running action. Thus exercises such as chinnies, alternate leg 'V' sits and twisting sit-ups are far more useful.

The same applies to the leg work. Squats and squat jumps do not work the legs in a movement closely related to running. Therefore we must use some more closely allied leg exercises.

### Step-Up Drives with Rear Leg Straight

These can be performed on the flat or on a bench (bench step-up drives) of maximum height 50cm. In this latter variation a higher bench (for the average person) leads to excessive rotation at the sacroiliac joint and may cause injury. A light resistance (maximum 20–50kg) is held firmly on the back of the shoulders. The athlete stands with knees bent (at about 120–130 degrees) and one foot slightly behind the other. A drive-up then follows, bringing the trailing knee up in front, as in an exaggerated sprint action. As the drive is completed the driving leg (the one in contact with the ground) is extended on to the toe. There should be no flexion at the hips at the high point of the

Figs 113-115 Step-up drives with rear leg straight.

Figs 116–118 Narrow stance split squat jumps.

movement. The reverse action is then completed and a slight pause is taken before the next repetition is attempted. It is best to exercise each leg separately (one set on the right leg and then one on the left). This exercise is excellent for specific leg strengthening for runners and athletes in events that contain an element of running.

## Split Squat Jumps

These may be performed with the feet either wide apart or closer together. The latter is most effective because, when the feet are wide, it is far more difficult to get an efficient drive, and there is a tendency to overstretch. In the narrower version the feet are no more than heel to toe apart and the bend is as low as possible without rounding the back. The eyes are kept parallel with the ground at all times during the exercise. Only light resistance should be used, probably in the region of 10–30kg. The drive upwards is vigorous with special emphasis being put on ankle extension and light landing. If the athlete can only land heavily, he or she is not capable of performing the exercise with any resistance. A period of working with just the body weight should therefore be adopted.

## Pulley Hip-Flexor Pull-Throughs

The strap is firmly attached to the ankle from the low pulley of a wall or free-standing stack system. The athlete faces away from the machine and with a slight lean forward, the knee is stretched backwards and then pulled through to the maximum forward position, as in the running movement. The leg is moved in a pattern closest to sprinting so that the hip flexor muscle system is worked effectively.

This exercise strengthens the knee pull-through in running. The resistance used should only be sufficient to make the

ii

iii

i

Figs 119–121 Pulley hip-flexor pull-throughs.

movement difficult but not unnatural. The repetitions will therefore be high and should relate fairly closely to the number of strides in the event being trained for.

## Pulley Hamstring Pull-Throughs

This exercise is in essence the opposite of the hip flexor pull-through. The same machine is used and the athlete faces it. The leg is brought forward and then swept backwards again, as in the running action. This means that the exercise is highly specific to the muscles involved in this part of the running action. It strengthens the back of the leg together with the gluteus group and the lower back. The resistance is kept fairly low to make sure that not too much stress is placed on the joints and that the movement does not vary much from the sprint action. Performed as a high-repetition exercise, it is an excellent way to strengthen those muscles that are otherwise rather difficult to work in a coordinated fashion.

Figs 122–124 Pulley hamstring pull-throughs.

## Dumbell Sprint Arm Action

This exercise is usually performed with dumbbell bars or weight discs (about 1.25–2.5kg). A split stance is adopted for stability and the arms moved over an extended range, mimicking the sprint arm action. Because of the light resistance, the repetitions should be high and relate broadly to the number of strides in the athlete's event. The position of the feet is alternated each set so that there is no bias in the exercise. This is an excellent movement for

Figs 125–127 Dumbell sprint arm action.

developing arm and shoulder power and relates much more closely to the sprint than do activities such as speed ball. In addition, the speed and range of movement may be varied according to the event requirement.

## HURDLING

The hurdler is a technical sprinter. The events require all the assets of the sprinter or quarter-miler together with the technical skill that can make the obstacles look like mere trifles in the way of the run. Such athletes as Jackson, Gunnell and Moses are the best examples, not only because of their obvious speed, but also their great technical strength. The hurdler must be strong since he or she has to move the whole body through the air in an efficient and rapid hurdling action if success is to be forthcoming. Therefore one would expect the hurdlers to spend more time in the gym than the flat runners.

Over and above the sprinter's strength work, the hurdler must have extra mid-region strength, and hip and leg power, to add to the flexibility needed for efficient technique. The specific work must therefore relate closely to the style of the athlete and can be developed as strengths and weaknesses become obvious. Two excellent exercises are described below, but there are many more available.

### Lunges

Lunges are a leg exercise that puts considerable stress on the muscles around the knee, as well as the hamstrings, gluteus group and lower back. Because this is a single-leg exercise, they are most useful for the hurdler who must be strong to cope with the landing after flight over the hurdles.

The exercise is performed with a light resistance (10–30kg) and emphasis must be placed on working on the toes at all times. The resistance is in the form of a barbell across the back of the shoulders and must be held firmly in place during the exercise. The athlete stands with feet together, and balanced on the toes. One foot is then

Figs 128–130 Lunges.

placed well forward (about 1–1.3m). As the foot lands, the knee is flexed and then straightened rapidly to drive the body back to the starting position. The drive is performed either steadily with the heavier resistances, or as closely as possible to maximum speed with minimal resistance to enhance the plyometric effect. The legs may be worked individually or alternately in each set, but it is essential to exercise both legs and not just the one used in the hurdle action. An imbalance in strength may lead to injury. Excessive lean forward with the body must be avoided as this will put undue stress on the back, but the position should be gauged by what is comfortable.

## Hurdle Sit-Ups

This is an exercise that strengthens the central abdominal, transversus and oblique muscles specifically for hurdling. The athlete sits on the ground in the hurdles flight position. From here he or she leans back with the arms moving as in the hurdle action. From this position the body is brought up and forward to the final position, with the stomach lying along the thigh. This exercise must be used only within the range that the athlete can handle without undue strain on the back. As strength is acquired, greater range can be achieved but must not be pursued regardless of the athlete's ability to handle the stress without non-muscular pain.

This exercise may be modified by making the movement circular as well as backward and forward. It is probably the best stomach exercise for hurdlers since it not only strengthens specifically but also contains an element of suppling as well.

## WALKING

Walking is often excluded from strength-training manuals, but nevertheless the

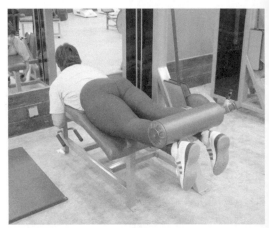

Figs 131&132 Hurdle sit-ups. (above)

Figs 133–135 Straight leg biceps curl. (Right)

walkers need special attributes to perform well. These particularly include strong hamstrings to pull the feet powerfully backwards during the exaggerated motion that is part of the walker's technique.

## Straight Leg Biceps Curl

The normal leg biceps curl is performed by lying flat on the bench and bending the knees to pull the weight in an arc towards the buttocks. A more specific way of doing this for walkers is to keep the legs straight and pull up by contracting the lower back, gluteus group and hamstrings. The movement can only be short range if performed on a leg extension machine, but can be extended if weighted boots are used and the legs are allowed to move lower towards the ground off the edge of a bench. The shoulders must be held flat as for the normal leg biceps curl movement. Only light resistance should be used, although there is a wide variation in strength levels from athlete to athlete.

## Alternate Leg 'V' Sits

This is an excellent mid-region exercise and can be used not only for walkers but in all event programmes. The athlete lies on the ground with arms and legs stretched out. One leg is raised and the athlete sits up and touches the foot with both hands. That leg is then lowered and the body returned to the ground. The leg is then lifted, hands again touching it. Within a short practice time the athlete can develop a rhythm in the exercise. It is important that the hands actually touch the feet as this gives maximum use of the abdominal muscles and hip flexors during the exercise. To make it slightly more difficult, light strap weights can be attached to the ankles and wrists, but generally, as this is a high repetition exercise, these are not used.

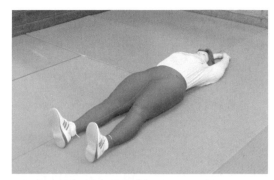

Figs 136–139 Alternate leg 'V' sits.

# CHAPTER 11
# Specific Event Exercises for Jumps and Pole Vault

The athletes in the jumping events are probably the most prone to injury in any group. This is not only because of the nature of the events but also because the conditioning needed is so demanding that many athletes tend to ignore the exercises that would provide preventive strength when things go wrong. Apart from the general strength work discussed in previous chapters, a considerable amount of specific work is needed to allow improvement to be made technically. The specific strength work should contain considerable plyometric content. The following exercises are a range of those that can be used. There are many more, but those discussed are some of the most easily performed.

## THE EXERCISES DESCRIBED

### Bench Step-Up Drives

This is a safer version of single-legged driving work than the heavy step-ups that tend to cause back problems in certain athletes. The bench used should be solid and no more than 30 to 50cm high; anything higher than this causes excessive hip displacement with its subsequent strain on the lower back. Resistance, in the form of a barbell held on the back of the shoulders, should be in the range 10–30kg. This is sufficient to make the exercise hard without causing undue distortion of the pattern of movement.

One foot is placed on the bench and then the body is driven upwards and slightly forward. As this is taking place, the rear leg comes through to the front, as in the long-jump take off. The driving leg is extended on to the toes to complete the movement with an emphasis on not piking at the hips. The whole procedure is then repeated and each set is performed on a single leg only. The other leg is worked in the next set. This is because a rhythm can be built up with the one leg but tends to be lost if the legs are alternated. Care should be taken not to bounce excessively off the floor with the rear leg. This is an excellent exercise for strengthening the legs in a movement similar to the take-off position in all of the jumps.

Figs 140-142 Bench step-up drives.

## Step In Step-Up Drives

This is a version of step-up drives that is performed on a flat surface. The athlete starts by standing erect with bar on the shoulders. A step forward is then taken with a slight dip on landing, making sure the body is held vertically. The athlete then drives upwards to the toes in a 'take-off' action. The exercise builds strength in a forward and upward driving motion such as is used in the jumping events at take-off.

Figs 143–145 Step in step-up drives.

Low to medium resistance can be used, although heavier weights, because of the complexity of the movement, should not be attempted.

## Split Squats

This is one of the most effective and useful leg exercises available in the strength trainer's repertoire for jumpers. It is performed with a medium to heavy resistance in the form of a barbell held on the shoulders, with the legs in the narrow split position (one foot forward and one back). With the body held upright, the legs are bent and then straightened. This is done carefully and slowly to avoid undue strain. It is important not to over-stretch, and to begin with the resistance should be only as much as can be handled with ease. This should be in the range 20–50kg but can be increased when the athlete is confident of the movement. Not only does it work the leg-extending muscles, but also the hamstrings and gluteus group. It is most effective in developing power in the pre-take-off stride and in addition helps to develop balance under stress.

Figs 146–148 Narrow stance split squats.

The exercise may also be performed with the legs split into a wide base position. This is a more difficult exercise and should be used by those who have some experience of the narrow split squat lift. Less weight would normally be used for this exercise since it puts more stress on all the muscles involved. It is nevertheless a useful movement for jumpers.

Figs 149–151 Wide stance split squats.

## Plyometric Squat Jumps

This is an easily controllable plyometric exercise. The resistance can be varied at will, but some preliminary work with a light resistance should be completed before heavier weights are used. The bar is held on the back of the shoulders with some padding if necessary for the lightly muscled athlete. A stable, upright starting stance is adopted while the athlete stands on a low box or block. A little jump is taken off the box or block into the quarter squat position. On landing, the legs are extended immediately and a jump completed at maximum power. The starting position is then readopted and the sequence repeated. Each repetition must be on its own to make sure that the athlete is prepared for the effort. Sub-maximal effort will not be effective.

This exercise is probably the most potent way of developing plyometric strength since it can be adapted to any athlete, however weak, and is so easily controlled that the element of injury which is so often present with box and hurdle jumping can be largely avoided.

## Plyometric Narrow Split Jumps

These are similar to plyometric squat jumps but a slightly lighter resistance is used (10–40kg). The only significant difference is that the starting position is with one foot forward and the feet land toe to heel. The athlete should again try to achieve immediate response. The leg bend is usually a little less than in the squat-jump exercise. Full extension through the toes to full extension on both legs must be achieved.

## Calf Jumps

Calf jumps are another of the plyometric exercises that can be performed safely in the gymnasium. The initial starting position is the

Figs 152–154 Plyometric squat jumps.

Figs 155–157 Plyometric narrow split jumps.

same as that for the plyometric squat jumps, except that the athlete stands on the floor. The movement, however, is different. The legs are slightly flexed and instantaneously straightened so that mainly the calves are used to develop the jumping power. The extension should be attempted as soon as the legs are bent. This ensures that the calves and not

Figs 158–160 Calf jumps.

Figs 161–163 Alternate dumbell press.

Figs 164&165 Pole vault chins.

only the quads do some work. To begin with the athlete must focus on using the calves consciously, but after some practice this becomes a natural action.

This exercise is particularly good for all jumpers since the calves are the fundamental jumping muscles together with the quads. Much dynamic work must therefore be performed to develop the required power.

## Alternate Dumbbell Press

This is an exercise which can be used to develop strength in the shoulders and arms in a way that relates to a degree to the arm action in jumping. It is, however, highly dynamic, easy and interesting to do. The dumbbells are held at the shoulders and a solid foot stance is adopted. One dumbbell is then punched upwards and then the other follows as the first is lowered. In this way a rhythm is attained, and the weights and body move in a coordinated fashion. The resistance should not be so great that a rhythm cannot be attained, but after a while quite heavy weights may be used.

## Pole Vault Chins

These form a difficult but specific variation of chins in which the hands and body are held as they are in the pole-vault grip. The athlete then pulls the body up to the bar with the legs as at take-off. This builds considerable

strength in the shoulders and arms in a specific way. It is hard to perform and youngsters may not be able to achieve the full range of movement, but even partial attempts will eventually build the required strength.

## Shoulder-Stand Leg Lowering

The athlete lies on his back on the floor and holds on to a support just beyond his head. The next movement is to raise the legs and body into a vertical shoulder-stand position. The body and legs are then slowly lowered until the feet touch the ground. It is vital to make sure that the movement is controlled all the way down and the body and legs are kept as straight as possible until the heels touch the ground first. This exercise mainly strengthens the shoulders and abdominal muscles. Athletes not in good condition should not attempt it.

Figs 166–168 Shoulder-stand leg lowering.

# CHAPTER 12

# Specific Event Exercises for the Throws

The following exercises are a selection of those that can be used as specific strengthening work for the throwing events. They may also be used as assistance work in a general schedule or as a change from the heavy basic exercises. They are more complicated to perform well than the general exercises and should be performed only by those with the experience, confidence and conditioning to maintain good technical form. They would normally be performed with light to medium resistance and with middle-level sets and repetitions (such as four sets of ten or more).

i

## THE EXERCISES DESCRIBED

### Bent Arm Pullovers

This is a commonly used javelin exercise which works the shoulders, pectorals and abdominal muscles. The athlete lies on a bench holding a barbell with a narrow grip (30–40cm) on the chest. From here the bar is taken backwards over the head and down to the ground. The elbows are held as close together as possible during the whole movement. The bar is then pulled in the same position back over the head to the chest. The range should be the maximum possible since the javelin thrower must be equally strong over the whole range of delivery. This exercise has an additional suppling effect on the shoulders.

For the most advanced lifters, the hips may be raised as the bar is lowered and then

ii

iii

Figs 169–173 Bent arm pull-overs.

Figs 176–179 Javelin pulley pull-throughs.

dropped as the bar is pulled over. *This should not be attempted by beginners as it involves considerable stress on the back.* Sometimes it is necessary to have the feet held down, particularly during heavy attempts. This exercise may also be performed with a dumbbell held at 90 degrees to the normal axis (like a two-handed javelin throw).

## Javelin Pulley Pull-Throughs

This is a similar movement to the bent arm pull-over except that it is performed standing up using the lat pull-down machine. The athlete adopts a medium split position like a throwing stance. The bar is held forward above the head and allowed to move back over the head as far as possible. From here the javelin delivery chest, shoulder and arm movements are mimicked as closely as possible, while pulling against a moderate resistance (if too much weight is used the movement becomes too dissimilar to the throw). This is a good, specific javelin exercise and can be included in the schedule with worthwhile results. It has a positive strengthening effect on the final part of the delivery.

Figs 171&178 Shot press.

## Shot Press

As the name suggests, this exercise is for shot putters. The athlete takes up a position similar to that just before the delivery of the shot (medium split). A barbell is held at the shoulders. Both knees are slightly bent and then straightened. The bar is projected

Figs 179&180 Dumbell single-arm shot press.

Figs 181–185 Throw pop-ups.

forward and up, as in the shot delivery, but not, of course, released. Complete control must be kept over the bar and only light resistance should be used so that there is no risk of letting go of the bar.

## Dumbbell Single-Arm Shot Press

This is a similar exercise to the shot press but more specific. It is performed with a single dumbbell in the throwing hand. Alternatively, a pulley system may be adapted to mimic the real putting movement. This is useful since a more extensive movement can be performed which resembles the near complete delivery of the shot. Heavier resistance may also be used since there is no risk of hurling the dumbbell across the gym.

## Throw Pop-Ups

This exercise can be adapted to all the throws. In essence, it is a plyometric activity for the initiation of the delivery movement for each throw. For example, a shot putt glide followed by a little jump from the landing position. For resistance, a light barbell (10–20kg) is placed on the back of the shoulders. For the discus, a turn is initiated and the pop-up comes on landing. Similarly, a single hammer turn or javelin cross-step initiates the movement leading up to the pop-up on landing. This exercise can also be performed with a single dumbbell in the throwing hand if close specificity to the event is required. The core of the exercise is the reaction speed on landing. A slow response will be non-plyometric and therefore the maximum reaction speed must be attained for the greatest effect.

## Inclined Flying Exercise

iii

i

iv

ii

v

Figs 186–190 Inclined flying exercise.

Figs 191–193 Sit-up rotations.

This is the inclined variety of the basic flying exercise movement. It strengthens the shoulders, chest and arms in the plane of delivery of the implement. Medium resistance should be used, although initially light work will educate the muscles in the correct pattern of movement. If you are using the bench setup, as in the pictures, care must be taken to ensure stability of the arrangement. A standard inclined bench-press bench is not as effective since it allows only limited positions to work from. It is important to keep the arms moving in a vertical plane with the angle of the body being controlled by the angle of the bench. In addition, the dumbbells must be halted at the lowest point so that the movement does not become a swinging action. The angle of the bench should be close to 40 degrees for the shot and nearer 30 degrees for the discus.

## Sit-Up Rotations

This is an excellent exercise for strengthening the central abdominal, transversus and oblique muscles for all the throws. The athlete sits with feet fixed at the top of an inclined bench with the knees bent. At the start, no resistance should be used but after some experience of the movement a weight disc may be used, held edge-on to the stomach. From the central starting position, the body is rotated as far as possible to one side. From here the body is rotated in the opposite direction, again as far as possible. At first the movement should be steady and controlled, but when the athlete is used to it a more dynamic approach can be adopted. Care must be always be taken to control the movement since excessive vigour can cause instability. The resistance used should be fairly light to start with (5–10kg), but heavier (15–25kg) as proficiency grows.

## Discus Hip Flicks

This is specifically a discus exercise, although it may also be used for shot and javelin. It entails the athlete's mimicking the initial hip drive in the delivery, using a light dumbbell. The athlete takes up the standing throw position for the discus and slowly rotates the body, taking the dumbbell round behind the back. As the rotation comes to an end, the hip is flicked in by rotating the foot quickly. The dumbbell will resist the rotation of the upper body, thus educating the thrower in how the delivery should feel. That is, the foot turning first, followed by the hip, the shoulder and then the arm.

Figs 197&198 Narrow grip snatch.

Figs 194–196 Discus hip flicks.

Figs 199–201 Dips.

## Narrow Grip Snatch

This is an excellent exercise for the hammer throwers. It is fundamentally the narrow hand-grip version of the normal power snatch. It is closely related to the delivery in the hammer since the whole two-handed movement is executed over the maximum possible range of movement, from near the ground to arms fully extended. Once the basic power snatch has been mastered, this alternative can be attempted, but bear in mind that less weight can be used since the bar must be raised much higher above the ground. The bar in this exercise should be lifted dynamically and arms and body fully extended as if throwing the weight above the head. There should be no dip on catching as the object is full extension to the end position.

The exercise strengthens virtually all the pulling muscles in the body to some extent and is therefore one of the best that can be performed.

## Dips

This is an old, traditional exercise, but nevertheless excellent for all-round shoulder and arm strengthening. It is important to do the movement correctly as there are several ways of cheating to make it easier. The starting point should be with the arms fully extended, gripping the dipping bars firmly. From here the body is lowered vertically until the chin is level with the hands. At this point the arms should be flexed to about 90 degrees. From here the arms are used to push the body, with no leg swinging to full extension. This full range movement will give great strength to the muscles involved. The exercise can be performed with a weight attached to the waist for extra resistance. Great care should be taken to control the movement and avoid forward and backward rocking since this causes undue stress on the shoulder joints and wrists.

## Rotating Dumbbell Snatch

This is an excellent exercise for the discus, shot and hammer. The athlete crouches down with a dumbbell placed on the ground behind the heels. At first only a light resistance should be used, which can be easily controlled. When the athlete becomes proficient, greater resistance can be used. To adopt the starting

Figs 202&203 Rotating dumbell snatch.

position, the body must be rotated towards the dumbbell. From here the weight is pulled above the head in one clean, rotating movement. Excessive rotation should be avoided since this makes the catching of the weight above the head difficult. Good control must be maintained throughout the movement. It is an excellent exercise, particularly for the back and shoulders. Because of the range of movement, it enhances the ability to perform coordinated movements more closely related to the throws.

## SUMMARY

The exercises discussed above in this and the preceding chapter are only a few examples of the multifarious possibilities available. The importance of specific strengthening work is becoming more and more obvious as we learn more about how the body produces its best results. With a little imagination and an essential understanding of movement and muscle action, novel and useful exercises can be devised which will help to produce dramatic results from your training. Caution must be expressed, however, in the performance of over-complicated movements that can lead to injury. Remember that the simplest exercises are often the most effective.

# CHAPTER 13
# In Conclusion

This book has been designed to give a broad overview of the fundamentals of strength training. There are many ways of gaining strength and the methods and exercises described here are some of the most important and effective, but not the only ones. The road to understanding is paved with learning. Never stop examining what you are doing and change it in the light of new knowledge. Listen to everyone and filter out the useful parts, applying them in your own methods.

Strength training is logical. Start at the beginning and finish at the end. Too often injuries arise from missing out stages in the athlete's development. Never attempt to make progress too fast as this will always lead to problems even if, at first, good results appear to be coming. Always make the schedules specific for the event and the athletes, since they all have different requirements. There is no such thing as one programme that suits all.

Integrate your strength training into the total year plan and technical work for the event and remember that, as the athlete gets older and more experienced at training, less general work and more specific work needs to be performed. Also go back to basics often, since excessively complicated schedules tend to produce smaller results.

Strength-training sessions must be paid the same attention as all other sessions within the overall programme, and the athlete needs to treat them as such and remember to warm up and loosen before starting, and then to warm down at the end.

Finally, the first rule of the strength training is safety. *Safety always comes first*. Do not be afraid to stop athletes in mid exercise to correct technique. Always insist on the movements being performed correctly and do not put up with bad skills. To lift weights safely, the athlete must be clothed properly, concentrating on the job in hand and fully understanding and able to perform the movements being attempted. Ignoring these rules leads to injury, which, in the case of weight training may be severe. Insist on discipline and correct behaviour in the gym and never allow any fooling around. If you follow these concepts the progress of your athletes will be steady and effective. Ignore them at your peril.

Strength training should be hard but enjoyable. Strive to understand the methods yourself and even try out the movements if you have not performed them before. From understanding comes the knowledge to teach, and teaching is the only way to educate your athletes in the skills and techniques needed.

# Index